CONFESSION OF FAITH

The Works
of Saint Nikodemos the Hagiorite

ΟΜΟΛΟΓΙΑ ΠΙΣΤΕΩΣ
ΗΤΟΙ
ΑΠΟΛΟΓΙΑ ΔΙΚΑΙΟΤΑΤΗ

Κατὰ τῶν, ὅσοι ἀμαθῶς καὶ κακοβούλως ἐτόλμησαν
παρεξηγεῖν καὶ διαβάλλειν Παραδόσεις τινὰς τῆς
Ἁγίας Ἐκκλησίας καὶ ἄλλα τινὰ τῶν περὶ Πίστεως
ὑγιῆ καὶ ὀρθόδοξα φρονήματα
τοῦ ἀοιδίμου Διδασκάλου
ΝΙΚΟΔΗΜΟΥ ΤΟΥ ΑΓΙΟΡΕΙΤΟΥ
ΝΥΝ ΠΡΩΤΟΝ ΤΥΠΟΙΣ ΕΚΔΟΘΕΙΣΑ
Διὰ συνδρομῆς καὶ δαπάνης
ΤΟΥ ΠΑΝΟΣΙΟΛΟΓΙΩΤΑΤΟΥ ΚΥΡΙΟΥ
ΓΡΗΓΟΡΙΟΥ ΠΟΡΙΩΤΟΥ
Εἰς κοινὴν ὠφέλειαν τοῦ Χριστιανικοῦ Πληρώματος.

ΕΝ ΒΕΝΕΤΙᾼ

ΠΑΡΑ ΠΑΝΩ ΘΕΟΔΟΣΙΟΥ ΤΩ ΕΞ ΙΩΑΝΝΙΝΩΝ

1819

CONFESSION OF FAITH

by our Righteous God-bearing Father
Nikodemos the Hagiorite

Preface by Dr. George S. Bebis
Professor Emeritus of Patristics,
Adjunct Professor,
Holy Cross Greek Orthodox School of Theology

Translated by Fr. George Dokos

Uncut Mountain Press

CONFESSION OF FAITH

uncutmountainpress.com

Cover Artwork: George Weis

Scriptural quotations are primarily taken from the King James Version. The translator to better reflect the original Greek text has emended some quotations.

Publishers Cataloging-in-Publication Data

Confession of Faith — 2nd ed.
Written by Saint Nikodemos the Hagiorite (1749-1809)
Preface by Dr. George Bebis
Translated by Fr. George Dokos

ISBN: 978-1-63941-031-6

I. Theology
II. Orthodox Christianity

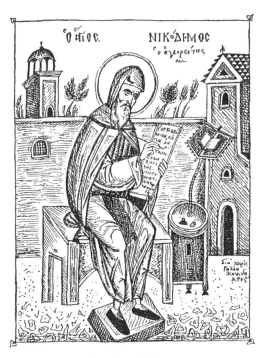

Apolytikion

Tone 3. Awed by the beauty.

Adorned wast thou O Father* by the grace of wisdom*
inspired thou appeared as* a trumpet of the Spirit*
and as a teacher of virtues* Nikodemos who speaks of God*
for to all hast thou offered* teachings of salvation*
and purity of life* pouring forth enlightenment*
by the richness of thy virtuous writings*
through which as light thou hast illumined the world.

"Always be prepared to give an apology to any
one that calleth thee to account" (1 Pet. 3:15)

"For with the heart man believeth unto righteousness;
and with the mouth confession is made unto salvation"
(Rom. 10:10)

Ο ΑΓΙΟC
ΝΙΚΟΔΗΜΟC

Ο
ΑΓΙ
Ο ΡΕΙ
ΤΗC

TABLE OF CONTENTS

PREFACE

I am delighted that my beloved student, the Reverend Father George Dokos, has given me the opportunity to write this preface to St. Nikodemos' Confession of Faith.

It is interesting that, after the general heading of this book of St. Nikodemos, it has a subtitle, and this subtitle reads *apologia dikaiotate*, meaning "a most just apology" or defense of the faith. Now as we know, St. Nikodemos became the subject of persecution, hatred, and jealousy because of his unending and strong defense of the Orthodox faith and practice, and he rightly claims that *phthonos*, envy, has become the ulterior cause of the attacks against him. And he consoles himself and gives encouragement to his followers by citing the examples of the great Fathers of the Church of the golden century of Christianity, that is, the fourth century: Athanasios the Great, Basil the Great, Gregory the Theologian, and Chrysostom himself. These holy and great Fathers of the early Church, although they were most pious and unshakably Orthodox, had been wrongly accused, incorrectly slandered, and sometimes persecuted for their steadfastness in the Orthodox faith and Orthodox practice. So St. Nikodemos claims, that if these great Fathers became the subjects of misunderstanding and slander and persecution, it was then impossible for Nikodemos to avoid the sufferings and persecutions they underwent. Thus, he says, that people accuse him and those with him not from what they know about them, but from what other people say about them. So they call them *Kollyvades* and heretics and un-Orthodox [*kakodoxous*]. St. Nikodemos, who is well versed also in ancient Greek philosophy and history, brings out the example of the great Athenian Aristides who was known for his righteousness and correctness, who, however, as Plutarch writes, was ostracized and exiled. And, as is well known, people agreed to his exile, not on the basis of their personal acquaintance with the just Aristides, but simply from what they had heard about him from others – from hearsay.

Following the example of what St. Peter the Apostle himself writes in his first letter, chapter 3, verse 15, St. Nikodemos writes that one must always be ready to offer a defense for the faith to all those who ask for it. In such a way they will close their mouths on account of the fear of God and because of the just punishment in the future life. Also, St. Nikodemos quotes the Apostle Paul who in his letter to the Romans, chapter 10, verse 10, declares *that with the heart man believeth unto righteousness; and with the mouth confession is made unto salvation.* Following these biblical groundings of his defense, he proceeds in a most positive and courageous way to proclaim his Orthodox faith.

First, then, that faith is founded upon the twelve articles of the common Symbol of Faith which begins, "I believe in one God." This Symbol of Faith is proclaimed commonly in the liturgical services of the Church or privately at home or in the cells. St. Nikodemos accurately quotes St. John Chrysostom who very correctly says that the accepted doctrines as well as the awesome Canons of the Church come directly from heaven (Homily 40 on 1 Cor.).

Second, St. Nikodemos confesses wholeheartedly all the other doctrines which the Catholic and Eastern Holy Church of Christ confesses and preaches concerning the most high doctrine of the Holy Trinity, that is, the faith in the Father, the Son, and the Holy Spirit, Whose Divinity is One, in accordance with the fifth Canon of the Second Ecumenical Council. He also confesses to believe in the profound incarnate economy of the Word, repeating what St. Basil the Great said: "We believe as we were baptized, and we worship as we have believed" (On Ascetical Discipline).

Thirdly, he confesses and accepts with profound piety the most holy and sacred seven sacraments of the Church which are Holy

Baptism, Holy Myron, the Holy Eucharist, the Priesthood, lawful Marriage, Repentance, and Holy Unction. He honors and highly praises these sacraments with great faith and piety because they contribute most necessarily towards the salvation of the soul. He fully accepts the grace and sanctification of these sacraments in accordance with the form and order which are performed and kept in the Eastern Church of Christ.

The fourth point according to St. Nikodemos is that he faithfully keeps the Apostolic Traditions which have been taught either by word or by letter by the divine and sacred Apostles. He and those with him remain steadfast in all those things which they have learned and which have been entrusted them, as St. Paul says in his First Letter to the Corinthians, in Second Thessalonians, and in the Second Letter to Timothy.

The fifth point is that he follows the traditions which have been designated from the successors of the Apostles, because the doctrines and the traditions of the Church do not contradict one another. God forbid! They are components one of another. Both of them have the same power and strength because the traditions of the Church are grounded upon the doctrines of the faith and, as St. Basil the Great claims in his 91st Canon, both of them have the same power and piety.

Sixth, as Orthodox, he accepts the sacred Apostolic Canons, the Canons of the Seven Ecumenical Councils, the Canons of the Local Councils, and the Canons of the Fathers that have been approved by the Sixth and Seventh Ecumenical Councils. He also accepts the minutes of those Councils.

Seventh, generally speaking, he believes and confesses all those things which the Holy, Catholic, Apostolic, and Eastern Church of Christ, the common spiritual Mother of all the Orthodox, accepts and confesses. And he avoids and rejects all those things which the Church avoids and rejects.

One of the most important controversies that developed on Mount Athos in the eighteenth century was over the service of the *Kollyva*. St. Nikodemos explains that *Kollyva* is boiled wheat, which is a symbol for the human body, because the human body is fed by and increases through the wheat. The Lord Himself (Jn. 12:24) and St. Paul (1 Cor. 15:36) also likened the human body to a grain of wheat. From this symbol the Church performs the service of the *Kollyva* both on the Feasts of Saints as well as at the Memorial Services of those brothers who have fallen asleep in Christ. St. Nikodemos writes that he and the others with him who are faithful to the canonical practices of the Church are slandered with the name *Kollyvades*, which is incorrectly addressed to them, since they follow the ancient traditions of the Church, which received instruction to perform the service of the *Kollyva* for those who have fallen asleep in Christ on Saturdays, and not on Sundays.

What are the reasons for the Church performing Memorial Services on Saturdays? One is because the Lord Himself was visiting Hades on the day of Saturday, freeing and loosing the bonds of slavery, while it was on Sunday that He rose from the dead. St. Nikodemos, quoting St. Dionysios the Areopagite (Letter Nine, To Titus), makes the point that those who perform Memorial Services on Sundays and not on Saturdays thus confuse the peculiarities of Saturday and Sunday. Another reason the Church performs Memorial Services on Saturday is because, in the Greek language, Saturday means rest, and all the souls that have fallen asleep have ceased from all earthly things. The holy Hagiorite also resorts to the liturgical texts and books of the Church which all clearly state that the day par excellence for Memorial Services is Saturday.

It should be noted that in a Patriarchal Encyclical issued by Theodosios II in 1772 (twenty-five years prior to the writing of the present work of St. Nikodemos), it was declared that "those who conduct Memorial Services for the departed on Saturday do well, as keeping the ancient tradition of the Church. And those who conduct them on Sunday do not sin." Obviously, there is a distinction made here. The correct and traditional practice is indeed to conduct Memorial Services especially on Saturday (and, as St. Nikodemos points out, on the other days of the week as well, except for Sunday, the day of resurrection and joy). Yet, by condescension, the Patriarch stated that those who need to hold them on Sundays for pastoral and practical reasons "do not sin." St. Nikodemos

explains here the two practices within the Church: *akribeia* or strictness and *oikonomia* or economy. He understands the need in certain
circumstances and places where the principle of economy and condescension may be applied, and he has no dispute with those who
implement the economical practice of the Church according to the
Patriarch's encyclical. The problem is that those who adhere to the
strictness of the Church's traditional practice of holding Memorial
Services on Saturday are being slandered by those who choose to
practice economy, even though the Ecumenical Patriarch clearly
stated that those who adhere to the ancient tradition of the Church
"do well." It should also be noted that, in order to put an end to
the persisting dispute over the celebration of Memorial Services,
in September of 1819, St. Gregory V, Patriarch of Constantinople,
issued an encyclical that decreed: "Memorial Services are to be
performed without distinction on Sundays and Saturdays, as well
as on other days of the week, in order to terminate completely that
dispute which arose long ago."

St. Nikodemos does not fail to mention the great theological
importance of Sunday, the Lord's Day. Sunday is the beginning of
the creation of the world, on which day the Father especially acted
with the co-operation of the Son and the Holy Spirit. Sunday is
the renewal of the Creation which the Son brought about through
His own resurrection. And thirdly, Sunday is the perfection of the
Creation, which the Holy Spirit performed, descending on Sunday
in the form of fiery tongues on the Apostles. Sunday is the eighth
day because it is counted after the seventh day, and it is the icon and
the prelude of the future age.

St. Nikodemos continues his Apology saying that he is criticized
for what he wrote in his book Spiritual Exercises, namely, that Jesus
practiced the art of carpentry. He defends himself by saying that
he did not come up with this on his own. Rather, following the
information given by Mark the Evangelist (6:3), and also according
to Matthew 13:55, the Gospel teaches that indeed Jesus did work
as a carpenter. He also brings forth the testimonies of St. Basil the
Great and St. Justin Martyr which attest to this fact. Jesus' labors, he

stresses, teach us humility and not to be idle, but to labor righteously in order to provide for our needs and to provide for the needy.

In the next part of his Confession of Faith St. Nikodemos speaks about the famous story of the Magi and about the miracles that took place in Persia on the day of the Lord's birth. Since he was also criticized by his adversaries for including this story in his book Spiritual Exercises (which he included in order to morally exhort his readers), he defends himself by saying that he based the story on information coming from a certain presbyter of the Church named Philip, on information gathered from the homily of St. John of Damaskos on the birth of Christ, and also on the history of Patriarch Anastasios of Antioch. These proofs may sound today somewhat insignificant. However, St. Nikodemos bases his information on manuscripts and books which he found in the libraries of Mt. Athos and of all the East.

Let us also add to this small prologue that St. Nikodemos was cognizant of some accusations brought against him concerning the divine Eucharist. His accusers stated that he believed that the divine body and blood of Christ in the Mystery of the Eucharist are passible and corruptible, and that the whole body and blood of the Lord are not present in all parts of the sanctified Gifts. But they are ridiculous and laughable, he says. He refers them to his book Unseen Warfare where he plainly states the opposite, that is, Holy Communion is really and truly the full body and blood of Christ in every part, and it is not corruptible, being the risen and glorified and immortalized body of the Lord. He further claims that the holy body and lifegiving blood of Christ are both real and spiritual. It is noteworthy that St. Nikodemos presented himself openly and proclaimed his innocence against the false accusations concerning the nature of the elements of the Holy Eucharist, declaring in front of all the brothers of the community of the Holy Mountain that he remains faithful to the teaching of the Church as far as the Holy Eucharist is concerned. The officials of the Holy Mountain promptly cleared his name confessing him before the entire community to be most pious and most Orthodox, "as is evident from his sacred and beneficial books."

St. Nikodemos finally asks his brethren to lift up their hearts and root out hatred against their brothers, because otherwise their life on the Holy Mountain, and all their ascetic efforts and toils will be in vain. If one does not love his brothers, he writes, his martyrdom is in vain. As St. John Chrysostom concluded, love, even without martyrdom, makes disciples of Christ, but martyrdom without love is nothing.

Every time I read the books of St. Nikodemos I am inspired by his humility, his love, his steadfastness in the faith, his faithfulness to the Canons of the Church, and his unlimited love for Christ, for His Mother the holy Virgin Mary, and for the Mother Church of Christ. St. Nikodemos, although he lived in the eighteenth century, still is contemporary, and I say this because even today there are people who do not like him and accuse him of being a westernizer and unbending. But we know that St. Nikodemos can speak to our hearts today and give us direction for a truly Christian life. Amen.

Dr. George S. Bebis
Professor Emeritus of Patristics, Adjunct Professor,
Holy Cross Greek Orthodox School of Theology

INTRODUCTION

Beloved, envy is a terrible and unsettling thing. It is always in motion and never ceases to effect its innate property, which is to ascribe blame to the blameless, to condemn the innocent, and to defame the most pious and most Orthodox as heretics and impious. As proof of this, it is sufficient to mention the examples of the great teachers and Saints of our Church: Athanasios, Basil, Gregory, Chrysostom, and the rest, who were most pious and most Orthodox, but defamed by their adversaries as impious and heretics.

So if these great Saints of the Church were not spared from envy and defamations, how would it be possible for us to remain above them and not suffer such things, we who are not even worthy to sit at their feet? It is nothing new, therefore, that we also are being criticized and defamed with slanderous names and called heretics by certain brothers who are moved by envy, spite, and hatred.

There are also some who, without at all knowing what the name *Kolyvas*[1] means, and without understanding the reason why we are being criticized and slandered, but because they merely hear that others call us *Kolyvades*, and heretics, and unorthodox, and other like defamations, they immediately follow the others in slandering us with such names. Therefore, they resemble those foolish Athenians who, being boorish, condemned the righteous Aristides and wrote

---

1 Translator's note: Throughout this work, St. Nikodemos consistently spells *Kolyva* and *Kolyvades*, etc. with one "l", and not two "ll"s, as is the current practice (today you will see it spelled *Kollyva*, etc.). A standardized spelling had not yet been solidified in his day.

on an ostrakon, or potsherd, against him that he deserved to be ostracized and banished from Athens, without having known him at all, but only hearing from others that he deserved to be ostracized and exiled, as it is recorded concerning him in the Parallel Lives of Plutarch.[2] So we rush to slander people, and resemble that popular and vulgar proverb which says: "When one barks, straightway another dog barks."[3]

Therefore, in order to set forth the truth, we are compelled to compose this Confession of our Faith by our own hand in this present essay, and to offer, in brief, an apology for what we think concerning those things for which we are unjustly criticized. For we hear the Chief Apostle Peter ordering: "Always be prepared to give an apology to any one that calleth thee to account" (1 Pet. 3:15), so that those who, on account of their passions, allege such things against us may shut their mouths, fearing God and the future retribution. And so that the other brethren who out of ignorance are scandalized and disheartened on account of what we have said may cease from being scandalized, on seeing the thoughts of our hearts revealed in word, in writing, and in print, for according to the Apostle: "For with the heart man believeth unto righteousness; and with the mouth confession is made unto salvation" (Rom. 10:10).

First then, we confess and proclaim and accept the twelve articles of the common Symbol of Faith, that is, those contained in the Creed, which we both personally and commonly read daily, in our cells and in the Holy Churches of God, if we happen to be present therein, for we hear the divine Chrysostom saying: "The dogmas, those fearful laws contained in the Symbol, have come down from heaven."[4]

Second, we confess and embrace all of the other dogmas which the Catholic and Eastern Holy Church of Christ confesses and proclaims, both concerning those things about the lofty and Trinitarian Theology, that is, the Father, the Son, and the Holy Spirit, being One Godhead, according to Canon 5 of the Second Ecumenical

---

2   Aristides, ch. 7.

3   Cf. Plutarch, *Moralia, An seni respublica gerenda sit*, 787C.

4   *On 1 Corinthians* 40.1, PG 61, 348; NPNF (V1-12), 244.

Council,[5] and concerning those things about the humble and incarnate Economy of God the Word. And may I repeat that which the great Father Basil says: "We believe as we were baptized, and we worship as we have believed."[6]

Third, we confess and accept, in accordance with Orthodox thought, the seven divine and sacred Mysteries [Sacraments] of the Church, which are: Holy Baptism, the Holy Myron [Chrismation], the divine Eucharist, the Priesthood, lawful Marriage, Repentance, and Holy Oil [Unction]. These we honor and praise in all faith and piety as necessary to bring about the salvation of our soul, and we accept the grace and sanctification of these Mysteries according to the form and order by which they are celebrated and safeguarded in the Eastern Church of Christ.

Fourth, we keep the Apostolic traditions which we have been taught, either by word, or by an epistle of the divine and sacred Apostles, and we remain in those things which we have learned and which have been entrusted to us, as the Apostle Paul commands us and all Christians in his First Epistle to the Corinthians (11:2), and in his Second Epistle to the Thessalonians (2:15; 3:6), and in his Second Epistle to Timothy (1:13-14).

Fifth, along with the Apostolic traditions, we also keep and accept the traditions of the Church, that is, those which have been ordained by the successors of the Apostles, for according to Eusebius[7] it was the opinion of the heretic Montanus, who flourished during the second century, to reject the traditions and customs of the Church. For the dogmas and traditions of the Church are not contrary to each other – God forbid! – but rather, they are components one of another. The dogmas of the faith constitute the traditions of the Church, and the traditions of the Church are founded upon the dogmas of the faith, and both alike have one and the same authority regarding the faith. Wherefore Basil the Great said: "Both of

---

5   *Pedalion* (Athens: Papademetriou, 2003), 162; *The Rudder* (Chicago: The Orthodox Christian Educational Society, 1983), 211.

6   *De Ascetica Disciplina 1*, PG 31, 649C.

7   Cf. *Historia Ecclesiastica* 5.16, SC 41, 46-52 (esp. 16.7, 47-48); NPN (V2-01), 229-233

these have the same authority with respect to the faith."[8] For just as large rocks are placed alongside small rocks and they both together constitute a foundation – for if someone were to knock down some of the small ones, at the same time he would also knock down the large ones – in like manner the dogmas of the faith stand alongside the traditions of the Church, and if someone were to reject the traditions of the Church, he would also reject the dogmas of the faith.[9] Wherefore Basil the Great again said: "For were we to attempt to reject such customs as having no authority, on the ground that the importance they possess is small, we should unintentionally injure the Gospel in its very vitals; or, rather, should make our proclamation a mere phrase and nothing more."[10]

Sixth, we keep and accept all of the sacred Canons of the all-praised Apostles, of the Seven Ecumenical Councils, of the Local Councils, and of the Holy and Godbearing Fathers, which are ratified in the second Canon of the Sixth Ecumenical Council,[11] and in the first Canon of the Seventh Ecumenical Council.[12] And together with their Canons, we also accept the Acts of these Holy Councils, for both have the same authority.

---

8   Canon 91 (*Pedalion*, 643; *The Rudder*, 854); *De Spiritu Sancto* 27, SC 17[bis], 480; NPNF (V2-08), 41.

9   Translator's note: That the dogmas and traditions of the Church uphold and depend on one another (and that one also must be faithful to them, no matter how much people criticize and reproach you), see Nikodemos the Hagiorite, *Pneumatika Gymnasmata* [*Spiritual Exercises*] (Thessaloniki: Regopoulos, 1999), 246-247. Concerning the defense of the faith and tradition, elsewhere he says: "If there is a discussion or debate about the faith and the traditions of our Church, then even the most peaceful and quiet person must fight against these, not with a disturbed heart however, but with a courageous and firm anger, according to that which Joel says: 'Let the meek become a warrior' (Jl. 4:11)" (*Aoratos Polemos* [*Unseen Warfare*] [Athens: Panagopoulos, 2003], 271).

10   Canon 91 (*Pedalion*, 643; *The Rudder*, 854); *De Spiritu Sancto* 27, SC 17[bis], 480; NPNF (V1-08), 41.

11   *Pedalion*, 220-221; *The Rudder*, 294-295.

12   *Pedalion*, 322; *The Rudder*, 428-429.

Seventh, and generally speaking, everything which the Holy, Catholic, Apostolic, and Eastern Church of Christ, our common and spiritual Mother, accepts and confesses, these things also do we accept and confess together with her. But whatever she rejects and denounces, we also denounce and reject together with her, as genuine and true children of the Church.

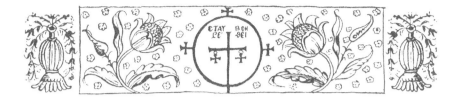

CHAPTER ONE

Concerning *Kolyva*

Having professed these things, we now will offer a brief apology concerning those things for which we are criticized. But before beginning our Apology, we thought it necessary to inform the readers about that which is called *Kolyva*. *Kolyva*, then, is boiled wheat, this being a symbol of the human body, because the human body is nourished by and grows because of wheat. Wherefore, our Lord also likened His divine body to a grain of wheat, as asserted in the Gospel of John: "Except a corn of wheat fall into the ground and die, it abideth alone: but if it die, it bringeth forth much fruit" (Jn. 12:24). And the blessed Paul said: "That which thou sowest is not quickened, except it die" (1 Cor. 15:36), for a dead body is buried in the earth and decays, just as a grain of wheat. From these things, then, the Church of Christ received the basis to make so-called *Kolyva*, both on the Feast Days of the Saints and for the Memorial Services of our brethren asleep in Christ, as Gabriel of Philadelphia says in his *Handbook*. Refined wheat, according to Blastaris, that is, boiled wheat, comprises *Kolyva*, and not unboiled wheat, mainly and primarily so that it may be eaten, on account of the miracle wrought by St. Theodore the Tyron, the originator of the *Kolyva*, on the first Saturday of the Great Fast, when he ordered the hierarch to boil wheat and distribute it to the Christians. And secondarily so that, through the boiling, the decomposition and decay of the bodies of those asleep be indicated, the *Kolyva* being a symbol of the bodies of those who have fallen asleep.

If someone were to say that *Kolyva* should be made from unboiled wheat and not from boiled wheat because boiled wheat will never be able to sprout, and because the bodies of those asleep which are already decayed will nevertheless be resurrected in the end, and therefore this is an inappropriate symbol and that the boiled wheat therefore does not symbolize a dead body, if, we say, someone were to say such things, we reply that this indeed is a most appropriate symbol, because just as it is impossible for boiled wheat to sprout by any natural means, by supranatural means, however, that is, by the infinite power of the God Who is able to accomplish all things, it is possible, altogether possible. Likewise, it is impossible for those dead bodies which have decomposed and returned to that from which they were made to be resurrected and enlivened by any natural means, but by the supranatural omnipotence of God it is exceedingly possible. Wherefore, the resurrection of the dead is confessed by all the theologians to be a work which exceeds all the bounds of nature.

CHAPTER TWO

Concerning Memorial Services

Now, having spoken about *Kolyva*, we first offer an apology concerning that for which many brothers criticize us, having no fear of God, calling us *Kolyvades*. And we say that this name is false and slanderously attributed to us by those good brothers, just because we keep the ancient tradition of the Church which is from above, and which from the beginning inherited the tradition to perform Memorial Services on Saturday for those who are asleep in Christ, and not on Sunday (by Memorial Services we mean those which are conducted with *Kolyva* present, and not the commemorations of names which takes place during the Divine Liturgy, for this is done for another reason, as will be explained). This is obvious from deduction, for the Church not only always performs the universal commemoration of souls on Saturday, and never on Sunday, as is apparent from the sacred *Triodion*[13] and the sacred *Pentekostarion*,[14]

---

13 Translator's note: The *Triodion* is the liturgical book of the Orthodox Church used from the Sunday of the Publican and the Pharisee through Holy Week, that is, it is used during the ten weeks immediately preceding the Sunday of Pascha. Its name derives from the fact of its inclusion of many hymns consisting of three odes instead of the usual nine-ode canons.

14 Translator's note: The *Pentekostarion* is the liturgical book of the Orthodox Church used from the Sunday of Pascha through the Sunday of All Saints (this Sunday being the one immediately following the Sunday of Pentecost),

but the Church also commemorates souls on every Saturday of every week, that is, she conducts Memorial Services for the departed every Saturday, as indicated by the sacred book of the *Parakletike*.[15]

For what reasons, then, has the Church always conducted Memorial Services on Saturday for those who have fallen asleep?

First, because the Lord's soul was present in Hades on Saturday, despoiling Hades, and loosing the bonds of the souls that were imprisoned there, as is verified by the divine John of Damaskos. For when he wrote to Kometas concerning the Holy Fast, this is what he said verbatim: "And so during these (the days of Great Lent) the Holy Spirit decreed, through the ministers of the word, that a fast be kept until the evening on five days of the week. But certain foods have been designated to be abstained from on Saturday and Sunday on account of the victory of the resurrection which we know to have taken place on Sunday. And on behalf of all the saints which have fallen asleep (that is, Orthodox Christians, who in general receive the name of 'saint'), an offering[16] is to be made every Saturday, as it has been ordered, on account of the Saturday preceding Pascha (behold the reason why we conduct Memorial Services on Saturday for those who have fallen asleep), on which day Christ bound the mighty enemy and pillaged his goods. This is the only Saturday on which those who are celebrating the joy of the resurrection should fast."[17]

So, for the reason given by the divine Damascene we have drawn this good conclusion, that those who do not perform Memorial Services on Saturday for those who have fallen asleep, but on Sunday,

---

its name primarily deriving from the fact of its inclusion of the fifty days between Pascha and Pentecost.

15 Translator's note: The *Parakletike* is the liturgical book of the Orthodox Church containing the weekly cycle of services, and used throughout the year. It is also commonly known as the *Oktoechos* because it contains the cycle of the eight tones.

16 Note that Saint John here appears to employ the word "offering" in a broader sense, that is, he uses it to mean those things which are offered at the commemorations of those who have fallen asleep, or simply, during what is commonly called Memorial Services, for the offering of the Mysteries [i.e., the Divine Liturgy] is celebrated daily.

17 *De Sacris Jejuniis* 3, PG 95, 69B-69C.

reject the reason offered by this divine Father and confound the peculiarities of Saturday and of Sunday, for it was on Saturday that the divine soul of the Savior was in Hades redeeming the souls there, and it was on Sunday that His soul, being united hypostatically to the Godhead, was out of Hades and united to His enlivened and resurrected body. The great Dionysios the Areopagite pronounces this general axiom: that no one should confuse the sacred symbols, because then the subjects, and the powers, and the orders which are being symbolized are also confused. These, rather, should be kept unconfused and appropriate to their respective subjects. He explains it this way: "One cannot use the sacred symbols haphazardly. They have to be explicated in whatever way that is appropriate to the causes, subsistences, powers, orders, and dignities of which they are the revealing signs."[18]

And in agreement with the divine Damascene, the divine Gregory of Nyssa says in his explanation of the inscription to Psalm 92: "Who does not know the explanation for the things which have been prefigurements of the faith: that on the day of the Sabbath the mystery of death would be accomplished? That according exactly to the Law, the lifegiving body was to remain motionless in the tomb on that day?"[19]

Second, the Church performs Memorial Services on Saturday because the word Saturday [*Sabbaton*], according to the Greek, means rest. So, because the souls of those who have fallen asleep have rested from all the things of life, they are accordingly and properly remembered on the day of rest, which is Saturday. This reason is confirmed by the *Synaxarion*[20] which is read on the Saturday of Meatfare,[21] as contained in the sacred *Triodion*, which reads as follows:

---

18   *Epistola 9, Tito Episcopo* 2, PG 3, 1108D-1109A; trans. *Pseudo-Dionysius: The Complete Works* (New York: Paulist Press, CWS, 1987), 285.

19   *In Psalmorum Inscriptiones* 2.8, PG 44, 521D.

20   Translator's note: The *Synaxarion* is the pericope read each day during the morning service of Orthros which contains either the lives of the Saints commemorated that day, or describes the special Feast or event commemorated that specific day.

21   Translator's note: More commonly known as Saturday of Souls or *Psychosabbaton*.

"We always (note the 'always') commemorate souls on Saturday, because Saturday means rest, according to the Hebrew. And as the departed have rested from all the things of life, we therefore offer supplications on their behalf on the day of rest, which indeed has been maintained to take place on every Saturday (as is prescribed by the sacred *Parakletike*, as we said above). On the present Saturday we commemorate and pray universally for all the faithful."

Note here what the wise Nikephoros Kallistos says, who is the author of the *Synaxaria* contained in the *Triodion* and the *Pentekostarion*. For when he says: "On the present Saturday we commemorate and pray universally for all the faithful," he indicates that on other Saturdays we individually commemorate our departed fathers and brothers, distinguishing between "universally" and "individually." This is also indicated by the ordinance in the *Universal Typikon*[22] [of St. Savvas] which says that the individual three-day and nine-day memorials which are held for any of the brethren who fall asleep during the period of Great Lent should take place on Saturday. And this is indicated even more clearly and more forcefully by the aforementioned words of the divine Damascene: "The Holy Spirit decreed through the ministers of the word... that on behalf of all the saints which have fallen asleep (that is, Christians), an offering is to be made every Saturday, as it has been ordered." Therefore, those arguments which some sophistically put forward are pointless and in vain, for they say that the universal memorials take place only on Saturday, but the individual ones also take place on Sunday. Furthermore, also note this as a logical conclusion: that those who perform Memorial Services on Sunday for those who have fallen asleep also reject the following saying from the sacred *Triodion*: "Sunday is not a day of rest that Memorial Services should also take place in it, as is Saturday, but Sunday is rather the first-fruit of the eternal mode of life," just as the Holy Church of Christ chants together with the divine John of Damaskos.

We, then, who keep the above mentioned tradition of the Church which conducts Memorial Services on Saturday for those

---

22 Translator's note: The *Typikon* is a book of rubrics, or liturgical instructions, of the Orthodox Church.

who have fallen asleep, and we who keep the aforementioned words of the divine Damascene and of the sacred *Triodion*, we, I say, are criticized and called *Kolyvades*. By whom? By those who transgress this tradition of the Church by conducting Memorial Services on Sunday. O earth and sun, and eyes which see justice! Is this a just thing that we suffer, we who should rightly be praised for this and be remembered as keepers of the Ecclesiastical Tradition? Judge dispassionately, we ask you, judge sensibly and with the fear of God in your soul.

That this is an ancient custom and tradition of the Church – to extend prayers and conduct Memorial Services on Saturday with *Kolyva* for those who have fallen asleep – is verified by many. First, it is verified by the very practice of the sacred and irreproachable monasteries of the Holy Mountain. The priests of these monasteries go to the cemetery with *Kolyva* every Friday evening and commemorate the departed. Likewise, every Saturday morning they liturgize at the cemetery chapel, commemorating those who have fallen asleep.

But someone might bring forth this argument concerning the subject of Memorial Services and ecclesiastical tradition, saying: "Dear friends, according to the arguments which you have presented, you have demonstrated that Memorial Services for those who have fallen asleep can only be conducted on Saturday, and on no other day of the week. But because it is not prohibited to conduct Memorial Services on other days of the week, it is therefore not prohibited for us to conduct them on Sunday." To such a person we reply: Beloved, you respond sophistically, whoever you are, for you ask in the beginning, and then you only take that which you want, just like those who are engaged in sophistries do.

We are not concerned, brother, with the other days of the week, but only with Sunday. For seeing Sunday set apart from the other days, even from Saturday, on account of the prerogatives which took place on that day – the resurrection of the Lord, the prefigurement of the resurrection of all the faithful – and on account of the joy of the resurrection, we follow the designations in the sacred rubrics, that Memorial Services for the departed are not to take place on Sunday. Concerning Saturday, we follow the abovementioned words of the sacred Damascene, of the sacred *Triodion*, and of the *Pentekostarion*, and we say that Memorial Services for the departed must especially take place on that day, because Saturday is the day of rest, but also because it was on Saturday that the Lord was bodily in the tomb and His soul in Hades, as we have already said.

We do not quibble concerning the other days, nor do they concern us, for we do not see the sacred rubrics or the ecclesiastical liturgical books concerned with them. Wherefore, whenever a Divine Liturgy is celebrated on these days, we also conduct Memorial Services for the departed, never distinguishing between the indistinguishable, except if there happens to be a Feast of the Lord or of the Mother of God on those days, for these are joyful, and Memorial Services are mournful, so they are not chanted on those days, according to the *Apostolic Constitutions*: "One should not mourn on a Feast Day."[23] We also see the rubrics saying the same things about Feast Days, as we will mention a little later.

No one can deny that Memorial Services for those who have fallen asleep are mournful and that they bring about sorrow. First, because the Church considers the departed brethren as sinners, and not as righteous, sin being the root and cause of sorrow and mourning because it separates one from God. Second, because the souls of those who have fallen asleep are considered to be in a dark and distressing place, and simply, in the prison of Hades, which is truly a place of sorrow and a cause for sadness. Wherefore, the Church offers supplication through the Memorial Services that the souls of the departed brethren be liberated from such a place and be placed in a place of light, a place of green pasture, a place of refreshment, wherein there is no sorrow and sighing. It is for this reason that all the living Christians who are present at the Memorial Services for the deceased wear mournful clothes, their eyes are sorrowful and filled with tears, and they supplicate and beseech the Holy God on behalf of the one fallen asleep with a grievous voice, saying: "Lord have mercy. Lord, grant rest to the soul of Thy servant." Third and finally, Memorial Services are mournful on account of their reference to death, the source of every sorrow and mourning. And if Paul

---

23   Book 5, ch. 20; SC 329, 284; ANF (07), 449.

says that we should not grieve over those who have fallen asleep (1 Th. 4:13), here, "those who have fallen asleep," does not refer to sinners (as those for whom we hold Memorial Services are considered to be), but it refers to the Righteous and to the Saints, as is evident by his words which follow, and as Chrysostom[24] and Theophylact[25] interpret this passage.[26]

But we hear what you are saying: "If death is the subject matter of Memorial Services for the departed, and this causes sorrow, as you say, it follows then that when the Saints are commemorated, and death again is referred to, this also causes sorrow." To these things we reply: The commemoration of the Saints is one thing, and the commemoration of sinners is another. For when the Saints are commemorated, even if death is referred to, it is referred to as having been conquered, because, being that the Saints are united to God by grace, Who is true life, even if they have died, they nevertheless live in God and in the grace of God, having only suffered that death which is physically according to nature, not that death which is against nature and spiritual. Wherefore it is said: "The Righteous live for ever" (Wis. 5:15). But during the Memorial Services for those who are considered to be sinners, death is referred to as the victor, because they, considered to be sinners, are reckoned as being separated from God, not having conquered sin while they were here, sin being the separation from God. Wherefore they suffered the spiritual death which is against nature.

We also draw this good conclusion (adding that which is more than necessary), inferring what is greater from the lesser. If sorrow is caused by the physically natural, and not spiritual, death of the Saints

---

24   Cf. *On 1 Thessalonians* 7.1, PG 62, 435-436; NPNF (V1-13), 352-353.

25   Cf. *Exposition of 1 Thessalonians* 4, PG 124, 1312A-1312C.

26   Translator's note: St. Nikodemos offers this same argument in his book *Kepos Chariton* [*Garden of Graces*], and adds the following: "And Paul confirms this [that he is speaking about the death of the Righteous, and not sinners] by his words which follow: 'For since we believe that Jesus died and rose again, even so, through Jesus, God will bring with Him those who have fallen asleep' (1 Th. 4:14),' for it is obvious that God will not bring sinners with Jesus in order to be united with Him forever, but only the Righteous" ([Thessaloniki: Regopoulos, 1992], 149).

(as evidenced by the tears shed by the Lord over Lazaros, and from the lament of the Apostles over the Protomartyr Stephen), how much more, then, how incomparably much more sorrow ensues from the deaths and at the Memorial Services of Christians who are considered to be sinners? For they are considered to be both physically and spiritually dead, having suffered that death which is against nature and spiritual, which is sin.

But let us return to the course of our thought. Second, the interpreters of the Canons verify the tradition of Memorial Services on Saturday, namely, the sacred Balsamon and the wise Matthew Blastaris. For Balsamon, in his explanation of the 51st Canon of the Holy Council in Laodicaea,[27] and Blastaris,[28] both agree and say that Memorial Services for the departed are to be held only on Saturday, and not on any other day during Great Lent. Take note, beloved, of that which Balsamon and Blastaris say here, for if Memorial Services for those who have fallen asleep take place only on Saturday during Great Lent, it necessarily follows that Memorial Services do not take place on Sunday. And because it is only on Saturday and Sunday that the Divine Liturgy is celebrated during Great Lent, and the abovementioned interpreters of the Canons say that Memorial Services are to take place only on Saturday, it is obvious that they exclude and eliminate Sunday. For if they were not excluding Sunday, they would have had to say that Memorial Services are conducted on both days, because the Divine Liturgy is celebrated on both days. What evidence is more evidentiary than this? What is more convincing than this testimony?

Third, the *Typika* of many monasteries verify this, especially that of Great Lavra on Mt. Athos, and that of Docheiariou, both of which dictate that whenever the memorial of the Founders of the monastery happens to fall on a Sunday, the Memorial Service is to be conducted with *Kolyva* after the ninth hour on Saturday, and after they have finished the memorial and distributed the *Kolyva* to the brethren, then they are to begin the Vespers of Sunday (their respective *Constitutions* are written further ahead). This is verified by

27   PG 137, 1409C-1412B.
28   *Syntagma Alphabeticum - T*, 5, PG 145, 149B.

the Breviaries, that is, the brief Codices, which contain the names of the Founders of the monasteries, and which are read in the narthex, but are not read at Vespers on Saturday evening. Also, if there is a vigil held on a Sunday, they designate that a *Liti*[29] be celebrated, so that the deceased are not commemorated.

Fourth, the *Typikon* of the famous Church of Protaton on Mt. Athos verifies this, which *Typikon* contains all of the individual *Typika* of the sacred monasteries of Mt. Athos, for the Protaton is the first chair, to which all of the monasteries of the Holy Mountain were subject. This *Typikon*, then, designates the following concerning Memorial Services: "It should be known that if a brother departs to the Lord during these holy days (of Great Lent, that is to say), his three-day memorial is not to take place during the week until Friday evening, at which time his memorial is conducted, and on Saturday the Divine Liturgy is celebrated (that is to say, with *Kolyva* present). His nine-day memorial is to take place on the following Saturday, whether it falls on that day or not. His forty-day memorial is to be conducted when those days are completed."[30]

This is taken verbatim from the *Universal Typikon* of St. Savvas, and from Chariton, and from Kyriakos, and from John of Damaskos. And because the aforementioned *Universal Typikon* says that the three-day memorials are to take place on Saturday, it is implied that these do not take place on Sunday, even if someone were to die on a Friday, resulting in the three-day memorial falling on a Sunday. Rather, the text definitely says that these are to take place on Saturday (and not, therefore, on Sunday). Likewise, concerning the nine-day memorial, it distinctly says that it is to take place on the following Saturday, whether or not it actually falls on that day, and not, that is to say, on Sunday.[31] Concerning the forty-day memorial,

---

29 Translator's note: The *Liti* [Λιτή] is a celebratory litany said especially on behalf of the living.

30 Chapter 116.

31 We said that the *Universal Typikon* designates that the nine-day memorial for the departed brother is to take place on Saturday, whether or not it actually falls on a Saturday, and not, that is to say, on Sunday. This is because through the weeks of Great Lent, on all the other days of the

it says, without specification, that it is to take place when the forty days are completed, and does not exclude the days on which it should not take place. On account of this the Godbearing Fathers of the Holy Mountain, who never differ with Savvas, or Chariton, and the others, on account of their sanctity, "comparing spiritual things with spiritual" (1 Cor. 2:13), according to the Apostle, defined the undefined, and expanded upon that which what was not communicated, and explained this obscure part of the *Universal Typikon*. Wherefore, by extracting the meaning they appended this part, saying: "And it is obvious that they (forty-day memorials, that is) do not occur during Holy and Great Week and during Bright Week, for if they (the forty-day memorials) happen to fall during these periods, they are not conducted (the Memorial Services, that is), except after the passing of the Sunday of Thomas. And because it is the tradition of the Saints to commemorate daily those who have departed from amongst us with Liturgies (note here, that these Liturgies are celebrated with *Kolyva* being present), that is to say, beginning from the first day of their death until the fortieth day, these Liturgies begin on the Monday following the Sunday of Thomas, and are continued until the forty days are completed. These Memorial Services are not conducted, however, on Sundays, and on the other Feast Days, namely, on the Wednesday of Mid-Pentecost, on the Wednesday before the Ascension (which is the leave-taking of Pascha), on the Thursday of the Ascension, and on the Monday of the Holy Spirit."

---

week, no Divine Liturgy is celebrated, but only the Liturgy of the Presanctified Gifts, and for this reason it is not permitted for Memorial Services to take place on these days. The Divine Liturgy is only celebrated on Saturday and Sunday. Wherefore, if it was permissible to perform Memorial Services on Sunday, considering that the Divine Liturgy is celebrated on this day, and considering that many of the brethren die during the week and many three-day and nine-day memorials fall on Sunday, if, I say, it was permissible, the text should have said that the nine-day memorial of the deceased is to take place on Saturday or Sunday, because the Divine Liturgy is celebrated on these days, as we said. But because the text designated that these nine-day memorials are to take place on Saturday, it is glaringly obvious even to a blind man that it means that it excludes Sunday, as not being permissible to chant these nine-day memorials on Sunday.

And see, O dearest reader, how much the Godbearing Fathers of the Holy Mountain adhere to strictness here, they who said above that it is the tradition of the Saints to commemorate daily the brethren who have fallen asleep, and they who struggle and fight so much to commemorate daily those who have died, being that they are lovers of the brethren, but who also definitely exclude Sundays and the aforementioned Feast Days, and who say with great exactness and discrimination that the Memorial Services for the brethren who have fallen asleep are not to take place on those days. What could be more obvious than this truth? What could be clearer than this ordinance? Or who can be found that has greater affection for one's brother than these Fathers of brotherly love?

The above witness of the *Typikon* of the Protaton would alone have been sufficient, being that it is the most inclusive, to convince everyone. But, to even further gain the trust of the readers, we bring here still more witnesses from various *Typika* of some of the monasteries of the Holy Mountain. We say, then, that the *Typikon* of the Sacred Monastery of Dionysiou, which is now a coenobium, identically quotes the above ordinance of the *Typikon* of the Protaton concerning, "What must be done if a brother departs to the Lord during Great Lent." It is written therein: "It should be known that if a brother departs to the Lord during these holy days, his three-day memorial is not to take place until Friday evening, at which time his memorial is conducted, and on Saturday the Divine Liturgy is celebrated…" and the rest. It then says the following: "Since it is the tradition of the Saints to commemorate daily those who have departed from amongst us with Liturgies, that is to say, beginning from the first day of their death until the fortieth day, these Liturgies begin on the Monday following the Sunday of Thomas, and are continued until the forty days are completed. These Memorial Services are not conducted, however, on Sundays, and on the other Feast Days, namely, on the Wednesday of Mid-Pentecost, on the Wednesday before the Ascension, on the Thursday of the Ascension, and on the Monday of the Holy Spirit."

This very same ordinance is also identically quoted in Chapter 119 of the *Typikon* of the Sacred Monastery of Docheiariou, and it would be redundant for us to write it again here, as we have already quoted it twice above, for according to the popular proverb: "If it is redundant to boil a turnip twice, how much more redundant is it to boil it thrice?" This same ordinance is also identically quoted in the *Typikon* of the Sacred Royal and great Monastery of Vatopaidi, which is written on parchment and found in the library of the sacristy, and which is inscribed as being that of the Studite Monastery.

The following is written in the *Typikon* of Great Lavra, the monastery of our Righteous and Godbearing Father Athanasios: "Concerning Memorial Services, if these feasts (that is to say, feasts containing Memorial Services for the Founders of the monastery) fall on a Sunday, this is how they are to be conducted. See to it, O time-keeper, that when these happen to fall on a Sunday, you must finish the *Kolyva* so that the Memorial Service can be chanted on Friday evening, and so that their names can be commemorated during the Divine Liturgy on the following Saturday in the chapel. This is most proper and orderly. Do this and do not hesitate."

And in the book of the Sacred Monastery of Docheiariou which contains the services of the Archangels and of St. Nicholas, it is written on the bottom of the page how the Memorial Services for the Founders are to be chanted if they happen to fall on a Sunday: "After the ninth hour (on Saturday) we enter the Church and first chant the service of the *Kolyva*, because the next day is Sunday. And after the dismissal of this service, we begin Vespers."

Let no one, upon hearing these *Typika* and ordinances of the monasteries of the Holy Mountain, disregard these as merely being exceptional, as some have foolishly dared to prattle, not having the fear of God. For we see in various books printed by our Holy Church that the Ordinances of the Holy Mountain are always referred to reverently and as handed down from the ancient Holy Fathers. In the sacred *Euchologion*, for example, where the explanation is written concerning, "What is placed to the right of the Holy Bread," these words are added at the end: "This order which we have just noted, is also the custom in all of the sacred monasteries of the Holy Mountain, which changelessly preserve the orders handed down from the ancient Holy Fathers, as those who are present there attest."

Also, in the service of the Great Blessing of the Waters, it is written concerning the prayer, "Trinity above essence," that this prayer is not said on the Holy Mountain. Furthermore, the following is written in the sacred *Horologion*[32] in the Midnight Office of Sunday: "One must know, that on the Holy Mountain of Athos, after the canon to the Trinity, the *More honorable* is chanted by both choirs."

Fifth, the designation which the printed *Universal Typikon* of the Church makes concerning the Saturday of Righteous Lazaros verifies the tradition of holding Memorial Services on Saturday. For on this Feast we see that, even though it is on a Saturday, on which day Memorial Services are especially held, as was said above, nothing is chanted for the dead, neither a hymn, nor a prayer. But instead of the hymns for the dead which are usually recited during the Midnight Office, only the hymn for Lazaros is said in the first stanza, and only his *kontakion* is said in the second stanza. When the time comes where the prayer for the dead is usually said: "Remember Lord those who hope in the resurrection," we see that the sacred *Typikon* instructs us to say, "Lord have mercy," twelve times (as usual), but not to say the usual prayer for the dead (but the preceding prayer, "I greatly magnify Thee Lord," is still said, for it is not a prayer for the dead).

But why? Because the Church numbers this particular Saturday with the resurrectional days. For this reason, the resurrectional *Evlogetaria* are chanted on this Saturday, and the "Having beheld the resurrection of Christ," is read aloud. What other argument could be more obvious than this? What could be more drastic to convince even the most headstrong person that, on Sunday which is resurrectional, Memorial Services for those who have fallen asleep must not take place?

And even if the resurrection of Lazaros did not actually take place on a Saturday, but his resurrection is merely commemorated on a Saturday, and still considering all this, nothing concerning the dead is said on that day, according to the designation of the sacred *Typika*, what mind, even the most dense and dimwitted, cannot

---

32 Translator's note: The *Horologion*, or *Book of the Hours*, is the liturgical book of the Orthodox Church containing the daily cycle of services.

conclude that even more, much, much more, nothing at all concerning the dead should be said on the day of Sunday, on which
day the resurrection of the Lord actually and truly occurred, and
on which day the common resurrection of all is typified, and on which
day it will actually take place? In truth, even seven year old children
could of their own accord and instinctively draw this conclusion.
For this reason, it is also explicitly written in the *Typikon* of Great
Lavra that on the morning of the Saturday of Lazaros, no *Kolyva*
is to be chanted in the cemetery chapel on account of it being a
resurrectional day.

That the resurrection of Lazaros did not actually occur on the
Saturday of Lazaros, but that the commemoration of the event is
merely celebrated on that day, ask John the Evangelist so that he
may teach you this. For he says in the eleventh chapter of his Gospel
that Jesus, after He resurrected Lazaros and heard that the Jews were
conspiring to kill Him, no longer walked out in the open, but went
to the city of Ephraim, and there He continued with His disciples.
The Passover of the Jews was near, but it is unclear as to how many
days prior to it Jesus resurrected Lazaros, for the Evangelist did not
reveal this. These are the words of the Evangelist himself: "Then
from that day forth they took counsel together for to put Him to
death. Jesus therefore walked no more openly among the Jews; but
went thence unto a country near to the wilderness, into a city called
Ephraim, and there continued with His disciples. And the Jews'
Passover was nigh at hand" (Jn. 11:53-55).

If the resurrection of Lazaros did not take place on the Saturday
of Lazaros, why did the Church of Christ accept to celebrate the
commemoration of the resurrection of Lazaros on that day? To this
we reply that there are two reasons why the Church does this. First,
because on that Saturday Jesus went to Bethany where they prepared a supper for Him, and Martha served Him, and her brother
Lazaros, whom the Lord resurrected, was one of those at table with
Him. Continuing from the above quoted words, the same Evangelist
John writes: "Then Jesus six days before the Passover (that is, on
the Saturday of Lazaros, for from that day until Great Friday, when
the Passover was eaten in the evening, six days are counted) came

to Bethany, where Lazaros was which had been dead, whom He raised from the dead. There they made Him a supper; and Martha served: but Lazaros was one of them that sat at the table with Him" (Jn. 12:1-2). The second reason for this is because on the following day, which was a Sunday, the entry into Jerusalem with palms occurred, and a multitude of the Jews gathered together and cried out that Jesus had raised Lazaros from the dead. For this reason, then, they greeted Him with palms, for they had heard what a great sign He had done, just as these things are attested to by the same lofty Eagle of Theology: "The people therefore that was with Him when He called Lazaros out of his grave, and raised him from the dead, bare record. For this cause the people also met Him, for that they heard that He had done this miracle" (Jn. 12:17-18).

Sixth, the Great Church of Christ in Constantinople verifies this. In the year 1772, during the reign of Patriarch Theodosios II of blessed memory, a Patriarchal and Synodical Letter was issued concerning Memorial Services in which was written the following verbatim: "Those who conduct Memorial Services for the departed on Saturday do well, as keeping the ancient tradition of the Church. And those who conduct them on Sunday do not sin." Behold, then, that the Great Church of Christ writes and confesses two things here. First, that to conduct Memorial Services on Saturday is the ancient tradition of the Church. And second, that those who conduct them on Saturday do well. So then, we who keep the ancient tradition of the Church and hold Memorial Services on Saturday for those who have fallen asleep do well, as keepers of the Ecclesiastical Tradition. Why, then, should we be criticized as *Kolyvades*, when the Great Church praises us as doing well? But notice that the Great Church does not say that those who perform Memorial Services on Sunday do well, but that they "do not sin." The one differs greatly from the other. In agreement with this, we add here that which Gregory the Theologian says: "For not every person unworthy of punishment is worthy of honor; just as not every person unworthy of honor is worthy of punishment."[33]

---

33 *Oratio* 40.23, PG 36, 389C; NPNF (V2-07), 367.

Seventh, the same Great Church of Christ again verifies this. During the reign of the most-wise Samuel, in the year 1773, the Church issued a Patriarchal and Synodical Letter in which it was designated that all the cells and sketes on the Holy Mountain must follow the direction of the sacred monasteries of the Holy Mountain with respect to how Memorial Services are performed and on which day they are customarily to be conducted. Both the cells and the sketes, as dependencies of the monasteries, are to conduct them on that day. Here is what the letter says verbatim: "We judge it proper that all those who are living a life of asceticism in the cells and in the sketes, as belonging and subject to the sacred monasteries, must unwaveringly follow and adhere to the order and custom kept in the monasteries concerning Memorial Services for the departed, that is, on whatever day of the week it is customary for the monasteries to conduct Memorial Services, on the same day they also should be conducted in the sketes and in the cells, without any disputation henceforth." And because the *Typika* and the Ordinances of the monasteries designate that Memorial Services be conducted on Saturday, and not on Sunday, as we said above, it follows that the cells and the sketes must follow the rule of the sacred monasteries, as their dependencies, and hold Memorial Services on Saturday, and not on Sunday. Eighth, the Church of Jerusalem also verifies this.

During the reign of Patriarch Sophronios of blessed memory, the Church of Jerusalem consented to and agreed with the above Patriarchal and Synodical Letters of the Great Church in Constantinople which were published under Theodosios and Samuel. For the aforementioned Patriarch Sophronios of Jerusalem signed both of them. And he not only signed them, but he also issued a letter of his own, in which he verifies the above letter of Samuel. When he was asked by the former Metropolitan of Lakedaimonia, Theophanes of blessed memory (who was at that time living in asceticism in New Skete), when the Memorial Services for his departed elder, the most-venerable hadji-Meletios, should be conducted, on Saturday or on Sunday, Sophronios answered him via letter that, concerning this, the Church designated that the sketes and the cells are to follow the Ordinance of the sacred monasteries concerning Memorial Services, wherefore, he should not seek any other Ordinance than this. We have both read this letter and transcribed it, as did the holy Makarios, former Metropolitan of Corinth, and of blessed memory.[34] Take notice, then, that Patriarch Sophronios of blessed memory consented to the ordinance concerning Memorial Services, that they should take place on Saturday, and not on Sunday. And if thereafter he issued another letter in which it was designated that Memorial Services may take place indiscriminately on Saturday and on Sunday, he did this because the so-called teacher Bessarion went to Constantinople and pronounced countless accusations against the brethren who were keeping the ancient tradition of the Church concerning Memorial Services, and he incriminated them as having heretical opinions. Sophronios, believing him as if he was speaking the truth, was deceived, and therefore the letter was issued. For if he had not been deceived, how could he so blatantly have deigned to say one thing, and then take it back and say something else? How could he who previously agreed with the ordinance of the sacred monasteries concerning Memorial Services, then say and write the opposite of that which he had signed, and the opposite of his own letter to the Metropolitan of Lakedaimonia? For this is not possible of any man, especially of a Patriarch, and of such a Patriarch who served like Sophronios.

As an aside, we also add these things here, that there are two types of governance found in the Holy Church of Christ. The first type is called strictness [*akribeia*], and the other is called economy [*oikonomia*] and condescension. It is, therefore, not anything unheard of, if the letter of Sophronios designates that Memorial Services for those who have fallen asleep may take place indiscriminately either on Saturday or on Sunday, for there were quarrels and disputes on the Holy Mountain concerning the subject of Memorial Services,

---

34 Translator's note: St. Makarios Notaras of Corinth once said: "I myself have neither performed nor will ever perform a Memorial Service for the dead on a Sunday" (Constantine Cavarnos, *St. Macarios of Corinth: Modern Orthodox Saints 2* [Belmont: Institute for Byzantine and Modern Greek Studies, 1993], 18).

and for this reason Sophronios, together with his Holy Synod, ex-
ercised care to pacify the disputes and employed the second type of
governance, that is, economy and condescension, and he designated
that Memorial Services may take place indiscriminately either on
Saturday or on Sunday. And what does "indiscriminately" mean?
It means not to discriminate between days, and not that one side
should force, or blame, or criticize the other, but that each side is to
be free to perform Memorial Services as it chooses. I will say it more
clearly. If you, brother, wish to have Memorial Services on Sunday,
holding to the economy and condescension of the Church, we must
not spy on you and criticize you for this, nor can we force you to
do them on Saturday. And conversely, if we do Memorial Services
on Saturday, holding to the strictness and ancient tradition of the
Church, you must not spy on us and criticize us for this, defaming
us with slanderous names. Rather, you should praise us. It follows,
therefore, that you must not examine us, in order to see if we are
doing Memorial Services on Sunday, or not. For both of these are
transgressors and lovers of turmoil, scandalizing the people.

Ninth and finally, the common practice and procedure in the
majority of the places of the world verify this ancient tradition of
Memorial Services, in which places the Orthodox Christian faithful,
as much as in Greece as in Russia (where the Memorial Services
for Emperors and for Imperial Leaders which happen to fall on
a Sunday are transferred to Saturday, as the Archimandrites who
come to the Holy Mountain from there attest), perform the Memorial
Services for those who have fallen asleep on Saturday, and not on
Sunday. And if in some isolated places of the abovementioned coun-
tries they are performed on Sunday, so what? This newer practice
is due to ignorance, or done for profit, or for self-satisfaction, or to
please men, or done on account of economy and condescension for
some reasons admitted by the Church of Christ, and for many other
like reasons, but they are not ancient and handed down from of old.
Thus, just as that which occurs rarely over time does not become a
law of the Church, according to Gregory the Theologian,[35] likewise,

---

35 "That which is rare is not the law of the Church" (*Oratio* 39.14, PG 36,
    352B).

that which occurs in certain isolated places and rarely is judged as inadmissible as having the authority of law.

But what do some say? "This tradition concerning Memorial Services is a small one in comparison to the large traditions that we transgress. So, if we transgress the large ones, let us also transgress this small one." To these people we reply that just as they do not criticize those who keep the large traditions of the Church, but rather praise them, likewise, they should not criticize but rather praise those who also keep this small tradition. It follows then, that we who keep this small tradition are not worthy of criticisms, but rather, of praise. Afterwards, this supposed small tradition becomes a large one when it is knowingly transgressed, and without any necessary reason, but with spite and passion, just as it is transgressed today on the Holy Mountain with such a spiteful attitude. For St. Dionysios of Alexandria[36] and Basil the Great[37] said: "The little things in life are not trivial." And some outsider preached: "The little things are not little, when they yield great things,"[38] just as small and pardonable sins become large and unpardonable sins when they are committed with contempt and spite.

And if someone brings up the prayer said over the *Kolyva* for the Saints, which is also said on Sunday, which reads: "It is unto Thy glory, and unto the honor of Saint (*name*), that this (*Kolyva*) is offered by Thy servants, and unto the memory of those who have been perfected in pious faith," if, I say, someone brings this up, we reply that here, "those who have been perfected in pious faith," refers to the Saints, and not to sinners. Wherefore the divine Chrysostom, in his Divine Liturgy, after the transubstantiation of the Mysteries, and after having mentioning the orders of the Saints, that is, the Martyrs, the Confessors, the Ascetics, the Fasters, he then mentions universally: "And every spirit that has been perfected in faith." By "spirits that have been perfected in faith" is meant all of the Saints, according to

---

36 Canon 1 (*Pedalion*, 545; *The Rudder*, 716).

37 *De Baptismo* 1.2, PG 31, 1525D-1528A.

38 Translator's note: This proverb is also quoted by St. Gregory the Theologian (*Carmina Moralia* 30, PG 37, 910A).

Cabasilas[39] and all of the other interpreters of the Divine Liturgy. Thus Basil the Great (in his Liturgy) also adds: "And every righteous spirit that has been perfected in faith." So how does "every spirit that has been perfected in faith," which Chrysostom says here, differ from the above prayer which says, "those who have been perfected in pious faith"? Certainly not at all.

That the phrase, "those who have been perfected in pious faith," in the prayer of the *Kolyva* does not refer to sinners, but to the Saints, is obvious to every careful mind for the following reasons. First, because it is impossible for a sinner and a Saint to be in one and the same body, holiness and sin being extreme opposites and their nature being unable to unite with one another. Here however, in this prayer, they would have it unite these two opposites with one another, because one and the same *Kolyva*, which is a symbol of the body of the Saint, then also becomes *Kolyva* of a sinner. But this is impossible to occur according to nature. Therefore, "those who have been perfected in pious faith," does not mean sinners, but the Saints. In this prayer, then, the rest of the Saints are referred to together with the Saint, like together with like, according to holiness. Second, because a common custom prevails, for after the prayer has been read over the *Kolyva* of the Saint, it is then taken away, and the *Kolyva* for the departed brethren is then brought in, and the customary prayer for those who have fallen asleep is read over it by the priest. Do you see, dear brother, how the two different *Kolyva* show that only the Saints are mentioned in the prayer of the *Kolyva* in question? For if sinners were also mentioned, what need would there be for a second *Kolyva*? But the *Kolyva* of the Saint is taken away during the commemoration of the sinners and the other *Kolyva*, which represents the sinners, alone remains. We must here again mention that which the great Dionysios says: "One cannot use the sacred symbols haphazardly. They have to be explicated in whatever way that is appropriate to the causes, subsistences, powers, orders, and dignities of which they are the revealing signs."[40]

---

39 Cf. *Sacrae Liturgiae Interpretatio* 33, PG 150, 441A-444C; *A Commentary on the Divine Liturgy* (Crestwood: St. Vladimir's Seminary Press, 1983), 83-85.

40 *Epistola 9, Tito Episcopo* 2, PG 3, 1108D-1109A; trans. *Pseudo-Dionysius: The*

But some say that Basil the Great calls the whole period of Pentecost a reminder of the anticipated resurrection in the age to come,[41] and others say that this period is considered as one day, so that if Memorial Services take place during the period of Pentecost, they also may take place on Sunday. To these things we reply that those who propound such things should also pay attention to what this same Basil says further down in order so that they may learn the reason why he said this. The Revealer of heaven continues: "For that one and first day (that is, Sunday), if seven times multiplied by seven, completes the seven weeks of the sacred Pentecost; for, beginning at the first, Pentecost ends with the same, making fifty revolutions through the like intervening days. And so it is a likeness of eternity, beginning as it does and ending, as in a circling course, at the same point."[42] Do you see, beloved, why the period of Pentecost is called either a reminder of the anticipated resurrection in the age to come, according to Basil, or one day, just as others have said? This is because the period of Pentecost begins from the brilliant Sunday of Pascha, and also ends on a Sunday, that is, the Sunday of Pentecost, and according to this it resembles a circle, which begins from one point and ends at the same point. In agreement with Basil the Great, Gregory the Theologian also says the following concerning Pentecost: "Thus the veneration paid to the number seven gave rise also to the veneration of Pentecost. For seven being multiplied by seven generates fifty, minus one day, which we borrow from the age to come, at once the eighth and the first, or rather one and indestructible."[43]

According to this calculation, then, the period of Pentecost is considered as one, but not as Sunday is actually in itself individually one, as Moses calls it when writing about the six days of Creation: "And there was evening and there was morning, one day" (Gen. 1:5), and as the interpreters of the six days call it. The period of Pentecost is also not considered as one day in the same way as Bright Week is

---

Complete Works, 285.

41 Cf. Canon 91 (*Pedalion*, 644; *The Rudder*, 855); *De Spiritu Sancto* 27, SC 17bis, 486; NPNF (V2-08), 42.

42 Ibid; trans. NPNF (V2-08), 42.

43 *Oratio* 41.2, PG 36, 432A-432B; trans. NPNF (V2-07), 379.

considered as one day. Not at all. For during all of Bright Week the entire Service of the Resurrection is time and again chanted, just as it is chanted on the brilliant day of Pascha, and there is no fasting whatsoever during that week, just as there is no fasting on the day of Pascha, and there are no Memorial Services conducted during that entire week. But during the period of Pentecost the Service of the Resurrection is not chanted, and there is fasting, and there are still more differences.

Wherefore, because the period of Pentecost is not equal in all respects to the one Day of the Lord, or to Bright Week which is considered as one day, the divine Fathers who determined the sacred types have designated that Memorial Services for those who have fallen asleep are not to take place on Sunday and during Bright Week. But during the period of Pentecost they are permitted to take place, both individual and universal ones. "The offerings," says the *Universal Typikon*, "and the Memorial Services (for those brethren who fell asleep during Great Lent), begin from New Sunday,[44] until the forty days have been fulfilled." It says that they begin from New Sunday, but not that New Sunday is also numbered among the forty days. God forbid! But what is meant by "from New Sunday" is "after New Sunday," in the same way as we are accustomed to saying, "He got up from dinner and did such and such," which is the same as saying, "After dinner," or, "After having eaten." And that this is the true meaning of this statement of the *Typikon*, we have the Godbearing Fathers of the Holy Mountain as witnesses, who wisely interpreted this passage. For they say in the abovementioned sacred *Typikon* of the Protaton, and in the *Typika* of Dionysiou, and of Docheiariou, and of Vatopaidi: "And it is apparent that it (the forty-day Memorial Service of the one who fell asleep, that is) is not to take place during Holy and Great Week and during Bright Week. For if it (the forty-day anniversary) falls during these weeks, it (the Memorial Service) is not conducted, not until after the Sunday of Thomas." Do you hear, that not until the Sunday of Thomas has passed are Memorial Services for the departed to take place? And

---

44 Translator's note: New Sunday is the Sunday after Pascha, also called the Sunday of Thomas.

again they say: "The Liturgies for them (those who have fallen asleep, that is) begin from the Monday of Thomas."[45]

Those, then, who also number the New Sunday among the days on which a forty-day Memorial Service can take place, distort and twist the sacred *Typikon*, and they truly have a passion for sophistry and deceive the people, desiring and persisting to hold Memorial Services on that day. And if they have not been shamed by the Holy Fathers, the true interpreters of the *Typikon*, they then should be shamed by the more ancient Gregory the Theologian who, in his *Homily on New Sunday*, shows it to be loftier than the brilliant Sunday of Pascha and calls it even more wondrous, for he says: "That Sunday (the Sunday of Pascha) was the day of salvation; this Sunday (the New Sunday) is the anniversary of salvation. And that Sunday is on the border of the burial and of the resurrection; this Sunday clearly belongs to the second genesis, for just as the first creation had its beginning on Sunday, so also the second creation again begins from Sunday, being the first Sunday after Pascha, and the eighth day after Pascha, being loftier than the lofty, and more wondrous than the wondrous, for it leads toward the condition on high."[46]

And if someone brings up the fact that during the Sunday Divine Liturgy we commemorate the names of those who have fallen asleep, to this we reply that there is a great difference between the names commemorated during the Liturgy and the names commemorated in the presence of *Kolyva*. For in the Divine Liturgy there is a subtle commemoration of the departed, without any mourning or lament, but in the Memorial Service for the dead with *Kolyva*, both the dead body of the person is present through the symbol of the *Kolyva*, and mourning and lament take place, as we said above, while there is also the chanting of solemn hymns. For what could be more solemn and more mournful than the hymn which says: "Whither all mortals go, singing a funeral dirge"? And it is forbidden for there

---

45 Note, however, that although the *Typika* designate that forty-day Memorial Services are to take place during the period of Pentecost, they definitely exclude them from taking place on the Sunday of Pentecost, and the other Feast Days, as we said above.

46 *Oratio* 44.5, PG 36, 612C.

to be mourning during a Feast Day, according to the *Constitutions* of the divine Apostles: "One should not mourn on a Feast Day,"[47] as we also mentioned above. So if there is not to be mourning simply during a Feast Day, how much more is it not permitted on Sunday, which brought us the unspeakable delight and the universal joy of the resurrection of Christ?

And if someone desires to learn a deeper explanation concerning this, let him listen with a welcoming disposition. The sacred and Divine Liturgy is a remembrance[48] and an icon of the entire incarnate economy of the Lord, for it contains His conception, His birth, His passion, His crucifixion, His burial, His descent into Hades, His resurrection, His ascension, His enthronement at the right hand of God the Father, and His second coming. There is nothing disorderly, then, or out of place, if during the Liturgy the memory of those asleep is carried out, either through the subtle mentioning of a name, or through the extraction of a small particle of bread on behalf of the deceased, for the Liturgy contains both the Lord's burial and His descent into Hades, where He bound the mighty enemy and pillaged his goods (which is the reason why we have been ordered to hold Memorial Services on Saturday, as we said above with the divine Damascene). But Sunday alone and by itself contains the mystery of the Lord's resurrection, and also therefore the common resurrection of all men, for Sunday is a type of the future age, as superseding the Jewish Sabbath, according to Basil the Great, and according to the first Canon of Theophilos.[49] So for this reason it has been appointed that Memorial Services not be chanted on Sunday, in order that this abuse may not be introduced by someone into the pure mystery of the resurrection, as much as

---

47 Book 5, ch. 20; SC 329, 284; ANF (07), 449.

48 Translator's note: Elder Sophrony (Sakharov) provides us with the meaning of this liturgical remembrance: "The whole Eucharist consists in 'remembrance'– understood not in the usual sense as a recalling to mind only but as an existential entering into Christ's world, into His Divine and human dimensions" (*His Life is Mine* [Crestwood: St. Vladimir's Seminary Press, 1977], 88).

49 *Pedalion*, 677; *The Rudder*, 904.

that of the Lord's, which actually took place on that day, as that of all of ours, which is prefigured on that day. And you heard above, beloved, where we showed from the sacred *Typika* that Memorial Services do not take place on the Saturday of Lazaros, because it is a resurrection, and that day is resurrectional.

On account of this reason, that is, on account of the Lord's resurrection, we are also forbidden to kneel on Sunday, as co-resurrected with Christ through faith. In agreement with this, the same thing is designated by Canon 20 of the First Ecumenical Council,[50] Canon 90 of the Sixth Ecumenical Council,[51] Canon 15 of Peter of Alexandria,[52] Canon 91 of Basil the Great,[53] Question 115 of the divine Justin,[54] Irenaios,[55] Epiphanios,[56] Augustine,[57] Jerome,[58] the divine Ambrose,[59] and Tertullian.[60]

But what do some say? They say that the former Patriarch of Constantinople, Kallinikos Zagoraios, wrote that Emperor Constantios held the Memorial Services for his father, Constantine, on Sunday, and that Theodosios the Lesser held Memorial Services for patricians on Sunday, and that some others did the same thing. And so they put these things of Kallinikos forward as some spear of Achilles. But what do we have to say as a response to them? That these things

---

50 *Pedalion*, 150; *The Rudder*, 196.

51 *Pedalion*, 298; *The Rudder*, 894.

52 *Pedalion*, 575; *The Rudder*, 754-755.

53 *Pedalion*, 644; *The Rudder*, 855; cf. *De Spiritu Sancto* 27, SC 17[bis], 484, 486; NPNF (V2-08), 42.

54 *Quaestiones et Responsiones ad Othodoxos* 115, PG 6, 1364A-1365A.

55 *Fragmenta, Deperditorum Operum* 7, PG 7², 1233A; ANF (01), 569.

56 *Expositio Fide* 22, PG 42, 825B.

57 *Ad Inquisitiones Januarii Liber Secundus, Epistola 55.17.32*, PL 33, 220; NPNF (V1-01), 314.

58 *Altercatio Luciferiani et Orthodoxi* 8, SC 473, 116; NPNF (V2-06), 324.

59 Cf. *Expositio Evangelii secundum Lucam* 8.25, PL 15, 1772C-1773A.

60 *Liber de Oratione* 23, PL 1, 1298A-1299A; ANF (03), 689; *De Corona* 3, PL 2, 99A; ANF (03), 94.

are no spear of Achilles, but rather a straw cane, unable to support those leaning upon it.

Because when we saw these letters of Kallinikos, we acquired the twenty-two volumes of the *Graeco-latin Byzantis*, and we found the abovementioned emperors, and the others which Kallinikos mentions, and after much careful research, reading each volume, we found nothing whatsoever in them showing that they held Memorial Services on Sunday. And not only did we find nothing of the sort concerning the people mentioned by Kallinikos, but we found no such thing concerning anyone. If, however, we had found at least one, we certainly could believe that the rest held Memorial Services on Sunday. But having found no one who did Memorial Services on Sunday, we conclude that Kallinikos added the "on Sunday" by himself, granting permission to those conducting Memorial Services on Sunday. And if he says that, while he was visiting Mt. Sinai, he read these things on some dense papers and parchments, he should have considered that the above volumes of *Byzantis* were transcribed and printed from those very manuscripts he mentioned. Wherefore, they should also contain those things said by His All-holiness. Moreover, those dense papers containing what he alleges would not only be found on Sinai, but they would also be found in the libraries of the sacred monasteries of the Holy Mountain, which are much more ancient than the monastery on Mt. Sinai. So then, Kallinikos, unable to substantiate those things he says from the printed volumes of *Byzantis*, and from the other books available to us, took us to the far away place of Sinai in order to make his words more convincing.

His All-holiness writes that, on the Sunday of the Forefathers, the following is sung in one of the hymns: "Today, O faithful, the day of the Forefathers, memorials are conducted." That sacred Head should have considered, however, that these so-called memorials are not the same as the memorials for those who have fallen asleep. First, the memorials mentioned in the hymn are only subtly said, while the memorials for the departed are said in the presence of *Kolyva*. Second, the memorials of the Forefathers, or of the Fathers, are said as for the Righteous and the Saints, and for this reason they contain nothing mournful, but those held for those who are asleep take place as if for sinners, being mournful and sorrowful, as we have already said.

Kallinikos adds that on the Sunday of Pentecost the prayers of Basil the Great are read, which refer to the memory of those who have fallen asleep. Thus, "behold where Memorial Services take place on Sunday." What wisdom! But His All-holiness should have gone deeper into things in order to also convince us. For the prayers which are read and refer to the memory of those who are asleep are read when? At the evening Vespers, when the Sunday of Pentecost has ended, and Monday has begun, for the Church of Christ begins every day from Vespers. Hence, "this line caught nothing," according to the popular proverb,[61] and this argument has no strength concerning the present subject of Memorial Services. But as it seems, His All-holiness would have the prayers of kneeling read on the morning of Pentecost Sunday, which is disorderly and improper, and which is not an ancient practice, but new, just as the sacred *Pentekostarion* of the Church bares witness, reproving him, and designating that the bowing of the knee is to take place in the evening, not in the morning.

We also add this. Even if a few of the emperors mentioned by Kallinikos held Memorial Services on Sunday, so what? Those few do not constitute the law of the Church, nor do they universally represent the Church, so that we might follow them, for, as we said above: "That which is rare is not the law of the Church," according to Gregory the Theologian.

So then, from everything that has been said, every one can see, even the most feeble-minded, as long as one has the fear of God in his soul and judges dispassionately and truthfully, that we, who keep this tradition of the Church concerning Memorial Services, which is attested to and verified by "so great a cloud of witnesses" (Heb. 12:1), should not in any way be criticized as *Kolyvades*, that is, as transgressors of the sacred tradition of Memorial Services. Rather, most certainly and by every right, we should be lauded as keepers of this tradition of the Church, and indeed also because, towards those who transgress the tradition and perform Memorial Services

---

61 Aristophanes, *Thesmophoriazusae* 928.

on Sunday, neither do we differ with them, nor do we quarrel with them, nor do we call them slanderous names. But neither are we pleased that this has caused disturbances and scandals and tumults, for we hate these things and reject them as our own sins. As many, though, as have criticized us and defamed us concerning this, calling us *Kolyvades*, are indeed worthy of every criticism, "their mouth being as an open tomb" (Ps. 5:10), according to the Prophet. They are foolish men, unlearned, having no fear of God, ill-natured, haters of the brethren, and enemies and destroyers of the common peace of the Church of Christ and of Christians, whether they be hierarchs, priests, monks, teachers, or laymen. Furthermore, they are defiant men and against the Great Church of Christ, subject to her fearful excommunications, imprecations, and curses, for she has everywhere in her letters, those of Theodosios, Samuel, and Sophronios, up and down with great thoroughness, declared and commanded and designated that those living in asceticism on the Holy Mountain make peace with one another concerning this unsettling subject of Memorial Services. As many, then, that are defiant and defame their brethren, are subject to severe penances and the harshest imprecations, and they are accused and unforgiven, and not to be loosed after death.

These Patriarchal letters were followed by the venerable and common Synaxis of the twenty sacred monasteries of the Holy Mountain, which issued a letter, sealed and dated on May 19, 1807, against a certain deacon of the Monastery of Esphigmenou who was prattling on and saying many slanderous things against the reverend Spiritual Father Papa-Hierotheos. The letter was read in the famous Church of the Protaton in the presence of everyone. The relevant passage reads as follows: "Let this example (of that slander- loving deacon) also bring the other slander-lovers and perjurers to reason, who have a heart trained in lies, and a tongue which loves to find fault and is moved by the devil, who open their rambling mouth and prattle on without the fear of God against the innocent and Orthodox brethren, calling them *Kolyvades*, and freemasons, and heretics, and unorthodox. For their false accusations cause fights, give birth to disturbances, incite hate, upset the common peace of the Holy Mountain, and uproot the love from their hearts, which is the sign and trait of the disciples of Christ and the head of all the virtues, without which, it is impossible for anyone to be saved. But if these people are not brought to reason, and do not cease henceforth from defaming the guiltless brethren, ascribing blame to the innocent, and the other defamations they hurl at those honorable men, let them know that they will be severely disciplined by our sacred Synaxis, locally and abroad, whoever they might be, as destroyers of the common peace of this holy place, and as creators of scandals and lovers of unrest, and as corrupters of the love for the brethren."

For this reason, we, the keepers of the tradition of the Church, are also able to call the transgressors of this tradition *Kolyvades*, and with every right, because just as those who make fabrics are called weavers, and those who make clothes are called tailors, and those who make shoes are called shoemakers, in like manner those transgressors should be called *Kolyvades*, and not those who do not conduct Memorial Services for the departed with *Kolyva* on Sunday, like us, but those who do conduct them on Sunday, for each person receives his name according to his work. Considering all this, we have never called them by this name, nor any other slanderous name, obeying our common Mother, the Great Church of Christ, and fearful of her excommunications, imprecations, and curses. But they irrationally, unwisely, and mindlessly call us *Kolyvades*, as truly disobedient and stiff-necked children of the Church of Christ, bringing her fearful penances and curses upon their heads. Indeed, those conscienceless people especially bring these things upon themselves because, as soon as they see some new brother who has recently come to the Mountain from the world, they immediately instruct him in their teaching: "Beware, brother, for here are found some heretics and freemasons, called *Kolyvades*, so be careful not to associate with them, do not even go near them, so they do not infect you with the poison of their heresies." O my God, how dost Thou endure their hatred for the brethren?

We conclude this chapter and say that, if nothing else convinces our brethren in Christ to desist from calling us *Kolyvades*, let the above testimony shame them, as well as the glory and the honor with which God this year glorified the two initial leaders of the ecclesiastical tradition of performing Memorial Services on Saturday. Namely, Papa-Parthenios Zographos of blessed memory, the common Spiritual Father of the Holy Mountain, whose sacred relics appeared fragrant when they were exhumed and transferred. Likewise, the former Metropolitan of Corinth, Makarios of blessed memory, who was residing on the island of Chios, whom the supreme providence of God glorified by the manifest miracle which occurred at his death. For there was a certain man named Korasios, who for a period of four years was suffering from four wounds on his hand which exuded some foul matter, and were deemed incurable by the surgeons on Chios. This man, I say, was wondrously healed after he placed his wounded hand upon the cap which the most aptly called Makarios[62] was accustomed to wearing in his home. This is exactly how this miracle was made known to the entire renowned island of Chios, and to the entire brilliant and great city of Smyrna.[63]

Do those who tenaciously transgress the ecclesiastical tradition of Memorial Services also have such supranatural miracles to show? Not one, not a single one. From where, then, and from what heavenly signs, or from what divine testimonies are we shown that they do well? Let the critics decide, having the fear of God.

Last of all, we seal the present chapter confessing and preaching with an open mouth, together with the Holy Seventh Ecumenical Council, the following: "If anyone rejects any tradition of the Church, written, or unwritten: Anathema."[64] Again we cry out with

---

62 Translator's note: The word (and the name) "makarios" means "blessed" in Greek.

63 [Note of the publishers of the first edition of the *Confession of Faith* (published posthumously at Venice in 1819)]: This is the only miracle [attributed to St. Makarios] which occurred during the life of the author [St. Nikodemos]. But after the writing of this book, many other miracles followed, being reported from other places, as contained in the *Life* of St. Makarios which is preserved in manuscripts on the island of Chios, which *Life* also contains a service to the Saint.

64 Beveridge, *Synodicon*, Tome 2 [Oxford: 1672], Act 8, 883. [Translator's note: Concerning the unwritten traditions of the Church, St. Dionysios the Areopagite says: "As for the consecrating invocations, it would be improper to set down in writing what they signify, nor could one publicly reveal their

the Council: "Every innovation and practice that is contrary to the ecclesiastical tradition, and contrary to the teaching and example of the Saints and of the Fathers of blessed memory, or anything that shall be done after this: Anathema."[65] This is also found written in the *Triodion* on the Sunday of Orthodoxy [in the *Synodikon of Orthodoxy*].

hidden sense and the power of God which is at work in them. Sacred tradition teaches us that one has to be introduced to them through processes of initiation which are not public" (*De Ecclesiastica Hierarchia* 7.3.10, PG 3, 565C; trans. *Pseudo-Dionysius: The Complete Works*, 257. See also ch. 27 of St. Basil the Great's *De Spiritu Sancto*.)]

65 Beveridge, *Synodicon*, Tome 2, Epistle to the Alexandrians, 606.

CHAPTER THREE

Concerning the Prerogatives of Sunday

As a supplement, we also set forth the following.

Brethren, we shudder when we think about the lofty and great and wondrous prerogatives of the resurrectional day of Sunday, which are these:

1) Sunday is the beginning of the Creation of the sensible world, on which day the Father especially acted, while co-operating with the Son and the Spirit.

2) Sunday became the beginning of the renewal of Creation, on which day the Son especially acted through His resurrection.

3) Sunday is the perfection of Creation, on which day the Holy Spirit especially acted, descending on Sunday in the likeness of fiery tongues, and enlightened and perfected the Apostles. Behold how much the whole Holy Trinity honored the holy day of Sunday!

4) Sunday is the eighth day: a) Because it is numbered after the seventh day, and it superseded the seventh day of the Jewish Sabbath, according to Athanasios,[66] Basil,[67] and Gregory the Theologian[68] in

---

66 Cf. *Expositio in Psalmum 6*, PG 27, 76C-76D.

67 Cf. *De Spiritu Sancto* 27, SC 17[bis], 484, 486; NPNF (V2-08), 42; *Homiliae in Hexaemeron* 2, SC 26[bis], 184; NPNF (V2-08), 65.

68 Cf. *Oratio* 44.5, PG 36, 613A.

their reference to the inscription of the sixth Psalm.[69] b) Because the resurrection of the Lord occurred on Sunday, being the eighth resurrection numbered after the previous seven resurrections, according to Gregory Palamas of Thessaloniki.[70] Three resurrections occurred in the Old Testament: one by Elias (3 Kg. [1 Kg.] 17:21-22), and two by Elissaios (4 Kg. [2 Kg.] 4:32-35; 13:21). Four occurred by the Lord: the daughter of Jairus (Mk. 5:41-42; Lk. 8:54-55), the son of the widow (Lk. 7:14-15), Lazaros (Jn. 11:43-44), and those who were resurrected on Great and Holy Friday (Mt. 27:52). Therefore, the Lord's resurrection is the eighth. c) It is called the eighth day because the Lord rose on the eighth day and appeared to the Apostles (Jn. 20:19), and again, after eight days, He appeared to them, Thomas being present (Jn. 20:26). d) Because all of the other Feasts of the Lord are celebrated only one time per year, but Sunday is celebrated every eight days, therefore it is celebrated fifty two times a year. Behold how much more exalted and supreme Sunday is over the other Feasts!

5) Sunday is one, as Moses calls it: "And there was evening and there was morning, one day" (Gen. 1:5). See further down for the relevance of this.

6) Sunday is an icon and a prelude of the future age. Wherefore Basil the Great, wondering why Moses called it "one" and not "first," says: "Thus it is in order that you may carry your thoughts forward towards the future life, that he marks by the word 'one' the day which is the icon of eternity, the first-fruit of days, the contemporary of light, Holy Sunday, honored by the resurrection of our Lord."[71] And Gregory of Thessaloniki says: "We call Sunday the new and first of all days. But Moses did not name it 'first,' but 'one,'

---

69 Translator's note: St. Ignatios the Godbearer also wrote: "And after the observance of the Sabbath, let every friend of Christ keep Sunday [the Lord's Day] as a festival, the resurrection-day, the queen and chief of all the days of the week. Looking forward to this day, the Prophet declared: 'To the end, for the eighth day' (Ps. 6), on which day our life both sprang up again, and the victory over death was obtained in Christ" (*To the Magnesians* 9, PG 5, 769A; ANF [01], 62).

70 *Homily 17, On New Sunday*, PG 151, 229B-232A.

71 *Homiliae in Hexaemeron* 2, SC 26[bis], 184; NPNF (V2-08), 65.

as superseding all the other days, and being a prelude of the future age: one never-setting day."[72] Gregory the Theologian, in his *Homily on Pentecost*, said: "Seven being multiplied by seven generates fifty, minus one day, which we borrow from the age to come, at once the eighth and the first, or rather one and indestructible. For the present sabbatism of our souls can find its cessation there, that a portion may be given to seven and also to eight."[73]

7) Sunday greatly surpasses Saturday, as much as the truth and the end surpasses the beginning, the type, and the shadow, according to Gregory of Thessaloniki: "As Friday is to Saturday, so Saturday is to Sunday, Sunday clearly surpassing Saturday, just as the beginning and the type and the shadow is surpassed by the end and the truth."[74]

8) The Lord will come on Sunday at the Second Coming. Wherefore the Godbearing Maximos said: "The appearance of the Lord will be on the eighth day (which is Sunday, for there is no other eighth day), that is, His Second Coming."[75]

9) The general resurrection of the dead will occur on Sunday, and not on another day. Wherefore Gregory of Thessaloniki said: "Sunday is so sublime and sacred, on account of the supremely blessed end and the hoped-for common resurrection of all that will take place on Sunday."[76]

10) The Righteous will enter into the perfect rest of that eternal and absolute life on Sunday, according to the same Saint: "On

---

72   *Homily 17, On New Sunday*, PG 151, 232A.

73   *Oratio* 41.2, PG 36, 432A-432B; trans. NPNF (V2-07), 379.

74   *Homily 17, On New Sunday*, PG 151, 229A.

75   From Niketas Herakleias, the Scholiast of Gregory the Theologian, *On Pentecost*. [Translator's note: Cf. Maximos the Confessor, *First Century on Theology*, 55, 56, *Philokalia of the Sacred Neptic Fathers* (Venice: 1782), 338 = PG 90, 1104B-1104C (*The Philokalia*, vol. 2 [London: Faber and Faber, 1981], 125). See also Peter of Damaskos, *Spurious Knowledge*, *Philokalia of the Sacred Neptic Fathers*, 631-632 (*The Philokalia*, vol. 3 [London: Faber and Faber, 1984], 192-193), and Basil the Great, *De Hominis Structura*, 2.8, PG 30, 49D-52A.]

76   *Homily 17, On New Sunday*, PG 151, 229A.

Sunday will be the perfect entrance of the worthy into divine rest, and the dissolution and restoration of the entire cosmos."[77]

11) Now, Sunday is an icon of the future age; then, it will be in truth the eighth age, for on Sunday the Second Coming will happen, as the divine Maximos said above, and the resurrection of the dead, and the delightful rest of the Righteous, as Gregory of Thessaloniki said. Many Saints say that the Lord, the never-setting Sun of Righteousness, will come at midnight on Sunday, as this is inferred from the Gospel passage which says: "And at midnight there was a cry made, Behold, the Bridegroom cometh; go ye out to meet Him" (Mt. 25:6). The reason being that once that Sunday is illumined by the rays of Christ the noetic Sun, it will never again see the evening, but it will be one never-setting day, without any successor, and eternal unto the ages of ages. Wherefore Basil the Great said: "The great day of the Lord (that is, the Sunday on which the Second Coming will occur, as we said above), not the day that the sensible sun will bring, but the day that the rising Sun of Righteousness will exceedingly illumine, will be one and unending, having no successive night, but extending forever unto the ages."[78] And again: "And only the Lord will be exalted on that final day of all days, which day neither night will interrupt, nor time confine, nor will physical light give a beginning and end to it, but it is one, unmovable, never-setting, and perpetual."[79] And again, in his commentary on the six days of Creation he says: "This day without evening, without succession and without end is not unknown to Scripture, and it is the day that the Psalmist calls the eighth day, because it is outside this time of weeks. Thus whether you call it day, or whether you call it eternity, you express the same idea. Give this state the name of day; there are not several, but only one. If you call it eternity still it is unique and not manifold."[80]

In agreement, the brother of Basil the Great, the divine Gregory of Nyssa, also says: "When the time of weeks comes to an end, the

---

77   Ibid.

78   *Enarratio in Prophetam Isaiam* 1.31, PG 30, 180B.

79   Ibid., 2.88, PG 30, 260B.

80   *Homiliae in Hexaemeron* 2, SC 26[bis], 182, 184; trans. NPNF (V2-08), 65.

eighth day (which is Sunday) will come after the seventh. And we call it 'eighth' because it follows the seventh, without however permitting itself to be superseded by any other number. For one day remains forever and the darkness of night will never interrupt it. For another Sun brings that day, which flashes the true light. When that Sun has illumined us but one time, as the Apostle says,[81] it will never hide in the west again, but after it has embraced everything, it ceaselessly sends its light upon the worthy, upon which no darkness will follow, and those who participate in that light are made into other suns, as the Word says in the Gospel: 'Then the righteous will shine like the sun' (Mt. 13:43)."[82]

And John of Damaskos says: "Eternal life and eternal hell prove that the age to come is unending. For time will not be counted by days and nights after the resurrection, but there will rather be one day with no evening (Sunday, that is), wherein the Sun of Righteousness will shine brightly on the Righteous, but for the sinful there will be night profound and limitless."[83]

All of these Fathers which have been quoted concerning the eighth and one day of the future age spoke of Sunday as the eighth and one day, according to Moses and the divine teachers, as was shown above. For this reason the Church of Christ also considers the whole of Bright Week as one brilliant Sunday in order to show by this that this entire seventh age of this present life will become one day, the eighth, that is, Sunday, which will be that eighth age of the future life.

We add a twelfth prerogative to the already mentioned eleven prerogatives of Sunday: the name of Sunday itself.[84]

Even if all of the other days of the week belong to the Lord, being His creations, none of them, however, bear His Name, for only that one and eighth day was worthy to be named Sunday [the Lord's

---

81 Cf. 2 Cor. 4:6.

82 *Ejusdem in Sextum Psalmum*, PG 44, 609D-612A.

83 *De Fide Orthodoxa* 2.1, PG 94, 864B-864C; NPNF (V2-09), 18.

84 Translator's note: Here the author draws out the meaning of the Greek word for Sunday, *Kyriake* [Κυριακή], which means "the Lord's Day," Lord being *Kyrios* [Κύριος] in Greek.

Day] after the Lord. First, because on Sunday, and no other day, the Lord's resurrection occurred. Second, because that day, apart from all of the other days, is especially consecrated to the Lord.

Do you see, brethren, the lofty prerogatives? Do you see the great prerogatives? Do you see the wondrous prerogatives of the resurrectional day of Sunday? These lofty and great prerogatives of Sunday, then, we fear to violate and to contravene. We fear to ascribe any dishonor to Sunday, the day so honored by the Holy Trinity. We fear to introduce the things of the seventh into the eighth. We fear to inject the shadow and the type of the Sabbath into the truth and the perfection of Sunday, as Gregory Palamas designated it. We fear not offering the proper honor to the icon of the future age, for "the honor given to the icon passes to the prototype,"[85] just as, contrarily, the dishonor given to the icon is brought upon the prototype.[86] For we tremble with the fear of God if indeed some others do these things, and we consider our fearfulness a safeguard. But if someone transgresses these great prerogatives of Sunday, and rejects the theologians and the holy teachers who say these things, counting them as worthless, "let him do what he will" (1 Cor. 7:36), for each is entitled to his own opinion. Let him not, however, defame us, but rather, praise us, who keep these prerogatives.

---

85   Basil the Great, *De Spiritu Sancto* 18, SC 17[bis], 406; NPNF (V2-08), 28.

86   Cf. John of Damakos, *De Sacris et Venerandis Imaginibus* 3, PG 95, 317B.

CHAPTER FOUR

That Our Lord Worked As a Carpenter

Some criticize us because we wrote in our book, *Pneumatika Gymnasmata* [*Spiritual Exercises*], that our Lord worked as a carpenter, that is, as a cabinet-maker or a woodworker.[87] For this reason we offer an apology here, saying that we did not say this of ourselves or make it up, but we followed the Evangelist Mark who clearly said: "Is not this the carpenter, the Son of Mary?" (Mk. 6:3), for the Lord was not only the Son of a carpenter, Joseph, as the Gospel of Matthew says: "Is not this the carpenter's Son?" (Mt. 13:55), but He was also Himself a carpenter. Those Jews who, according to Matthew, said He was the Son of a carpenter, also said, according to Mark, that He Himself was a carpenter. And see the abovementioned two Gospel passages to be convinced of that which we are saying to you is true. Wherefore, just as it is true to say that He was the Son of a carpenter (for all of the divine Fathers commonly agree on this, that is, that Joseph, the thought-to-be father of the Lord, was a carpenter, and that the Lord was the Son of a carpenter), it is also true to say that He was a carpenter.

8/ Translator's note: This book, written by St. Nikodemos and published for the first time in 1800 at Venice (and published seven more times since then), consists of thirty-four longer Meditations, thirty brief Meditations, eight Exercises, and eight Readings. It is to part two of the twenty-third longer Meditation to which he is referring here.

Basil the Great verifies this saying that, because the parents of the Lord were poor and provided for their family through the labor of their hands, it was also necessary for the Lord to labor in this fashion with them: "He was from the youngest age obedient to His parents (the Lord, that is), bearing with them every bodily labor meekly and readily. For they were righteous and pious people, poor and without even the bare necessities (the manger witnesses to this, that servant of the precious birth). Doubtless, they met perpetually with bodily labors and worked together to provide for their necessities. And Jesus was obedient to them, as the Scripture says (Lk. 2:51), always bearing the labors with them and showing ready obedience."[88]

Do you hear, beloved, what Basil the Great is saying here? Namely, that the Lord undertook every bodily labor, meekly and readily, together with His parents. Wherefore, because His supposed father, Joseph, was a carpenter, for this reason the Lord also labored together with him in the vocation of carpentry, lifting wood, cutting, sawing, and undergoing every other labor demanded by this vocation. How can you then, whoever you are, unjustly and wrongly criticize us for saying that the Lord labored in carpentry, when you can see that the Evangelist Mark himself clearly says this, as well as Basil the Great? But as it seems, you are greater and wiser and more able to judge than they, and for this reason you also criticize the Evangelist Mark, and Basil the Great. How great this foolishness and this pride is, consider for yourself.

This is verified above all by the divine Philosopher and Martyr Justin, clearly witnessing to this in his authentic *Dialogue with Trypho the Jew*, saying: "While among men, He (Jesus) was in the habit of working as a carpenter, making ploughs and yokes, by which labors He taught the symbols of righteousness and an active life."[89] He says namely that Jesus Christ performed the handicrafts of carpentry, and made ploughs and yokes for oxen, and through the yokes He taught men to observe righteousness and equality, just as the yokes

---

88   *Constitutiones Asceticae* 6, PG 31, 1356C-1357A.

89   *Dialogus cum Tryphone Judaeo* 88, PG 6, 688B; trans. ANF (01), 244. [Translator's note: St. Nikodemos references an edition of this work of St. Justin Martyr published at Venice in 1747, 196.]

have equality between them, and through the ploughs He taught men not to pass their lives in idleness and without handiwork, but to labor and work, just as ploughs do not stand idle, but till the earth when pulled by the oxen.

Do you see that you criticize us unjustly? Do you see that, according to this Saint Justin, the Lord of all deigned to practice, not the general, more honorable, and practical craft of carpentry (as we say in the *Spiritual Exercises*), but the most degrading, poorest, and most ridiculed type of carpentry?

Therefore, brother, whoever you are, desist from criticizing us unjustly, when you see that the Saints bear witness to what we said in the *Spiritual Exercises*.

Our Holy Father Epiphanios of Cyprus also verifies this. For in his *Homily on the Burial of the Divine Body of the Lord*, which begins with the words: "What is this? There is great silence upon the earth today," in this homily, I say, he does not simply call the Lord the Son of a carpenter, but clearly and openly calls Him a carpenter, saying: "Give me the dead body of Jesus the carpenter for burial."[90]

The Prophet-king David also verifies this. For when, in the Holy Spirit, he foresaw the poverty and the labors that sweetest Jesus Christ would experience during His sojourn in the flesh, in one place he said: "Poor and needy am I, and in labors from my youth" (Ps. 87:15). For according to Gregory the Theologian, Athanasios, Diodoros, and Euthymios, the interpreters of this passage, David prophesies these things from the perspective of the Lord, and perhaps the Lord here calls "labors," in addition to the schemings and plots made against His life (by Herod and the Jews) on account of those swaddling clothes, also the hardships He underwent while working as a carpenter, enduring the scorching heat of the summer and the frigidness of winter. This same David again said in another place: "Poor and in sorrow am I" (Ps. 68:29). This too David prophesies from the perspective of the Lord, according to Euthymios, and Cyril who says: "The King of all and all-perfect God was born from

---

90 *Sancto et Magno Sabbato*, PG 43, 445C. [Translator's note: The manuscript which St. Nikodemos had, simply read: "Jesus the carpenter," but notice that the edition in Migne reads: "Jesus the carpenter's son."]

a poor Mother, and not even in a house, but in a manger belonging to animals. He was wrapped in poor and contemptible clothes. He was left alone to walk without a helper. He did not even have a hut."[91]

And elsewhere, this same David said this concerning the Lord: "And he (Judas, that is) persecuted a man that was poor and destitute, and one broken in heart, that he might slay him" (Ps. 108:16), which the divine Hesychios interprets, saying: "The Lord was poor and destitute, for being rich, He became poor for us.[92] But His poverty was so great that He said: 'The foxes have holes, and the birds of the air have nests; but the Son of man hath not where to lay His head' (Mt. 8:20). This is excessive poverty."

And if it be necessary to verify this from the testimonies of more recent teachers, listen to what the wise teacher Eugenios Boulgaris says in his newly-printed *Ekatontaeteris*: "It is very certain that after the death of His supposed father, Joseph, Jesus practiced woodworking during this time (namely, from twelve years of age until twenty nine years of age). Wherefore He is also called a carpenter."[93] These things are underscored by the testimonies of the passage from the Evangelist Mark and by the abovementioned Philosopher and Martyr Justin.

And we are resigned to say that all of the Lord's relatives, who were called *Desposynoi* [belonging to the Lord],[94] had difficult and poor agricultural vocations. Wherefore the Emperor Domitian, when he went to Jerusalem to eradicate the race of David, in order to get rid of any hope of a coming Messiah, called for all of the relatives of the Lord. And when he saw how their hands were swollen and full of calluses from their laborious vocations, and learned from them that they were poor farmers, he dismissed them without disturbing them whatsoever.[95]

---

91 Translator's note: See also St. Basil the Great, *De Humilitate* 6, PG 31, 536C.

92 Cf. 2 Cor. 8:9.

93 *The First One Hundred Years After Christ the Savior* (Leipzig and Moscow: 1805), 36.

94 Cf. Julius Africanus, *Epistula ad Aristidem*, 5, PG 10, 61A; ANF (06), 127.

95 From Dositheos and from the newly-printed *Ekatontaeteris* (Eugenios Boulgaris, *The First One Hundred Years After Christ the Savior*).

But what do some say? "If we admit that the Lord had a vocation and a handicraft, we greatly demean His majesty." O the foolishness and the ludicrous ideas of those who say such things! Mindless people: If the Lord deigned to be born inside of a cave, and to be laid in a manger belonging to mindless animals (something which is not found in all of the stories of the world, neither of a child of the lowliest shepherd, nor of a child of the poorest and most dishonorable farmer), what is so unbelievable if the Lord deigned to labor in a vocation, something that is honorable and glorious? If the Lord deigned to serve His disciples when they were seated at table, not thinking Himself above this, as He Himself says: "For who is greater, he that sitteth at meat, or he that serveth?" (Lk. 22:27); and again: "The Son of man came not to be ministered unto, but to minister" (Mt. 20:28), what is so strange if He served His supposed father, Joseph, and labored with him as a carpenter? If the Lord was not ashamed, but deigned to wash (O infinite condescension!) His disciples' feet with His very own hands, even the filthy feet of that betrayer Judas, is it any more of a condescension for Him to have a vocation and a handicraft? And if the Lord deigned to carry the dishonorable wood of the Cross upon His shoulders, and to be crucified as a common criminal and a felon between two thieves and felons, how can anyone still think, even with the best of intentions, that it is demeaning and dishonorable for the Lord to have a vocation and a handicraft?

Moreover, you are the type of people who wrongly and erroneously think that a handicraft and a vocation is dishonorable and demeaning. For this reason, many of you, who were craftsmen, or tailors, or cabinet-makers, and then afterwards became rich, quit your vocation thinking it dishonorable, and then live idly and vainly in this world, and you are neither useful to yourselves, nor to others. But our Lord Jesus Christ, being far from your erroneous thoughts, did not think a handicraft and a vocation to be dishonorable. No. No. Because there is only one thing that He considers a dishonor, sin, and not a vocation. Wherefore, just as all of the other humiliations which the Lord experienced by becoming a man (as we said above) were not demeaning or dishonorable to Him, but, rather, were glory,

and honor, and majesty to Him, as Paul says: "And being found
in fashion as a man, He humbled Himself, and became obedient unto
death, even the death of the cross. Wherefore God also hath highly
exalted Him, and given Him a name which is above every name"
(Phil. 2:8-9), likewise the vocation and the handicraft which the
Lord practiced was not demeaning to Him, but glory, and honor,
and majesty to Him.

In truth, those people who say that a vocation and a handicraft
were demeaning to the Lord, clearly show that they are unspiritual
people, worldly, and people who do not have an evangelic and
Christian mind, nor do they know the reason and the purpose for
which the Lord came to earth. Wherefore, they would have preferred that the Lord remained idle, just as most of them sit idle.
And they would have preferred that He did not work and practice
a vocation, just as they do not work, but that He would get up from
His bed in the morning, fix Himself up, go to the bazaar in order to
learn the latest news from the newspapers concerning the emperors
of the world, and in order to learn what so and so is up to... But O
how deceived and mindless these people are! And O how far they are
from the knowledge of the Gospel and from the purpose of the Lord
Jesus Christ! The purpose of the Lord's coming to earth, brethren,
was not this. No. But it was to teach people to become humble, to be
poor, and not to sit idle, for according to Sirach: "Idleness teaches
much (that is, every) evil" (Sir. 33:28). The intent of the Lord was to
teach people by His example to practice a lowly and mean craft, and
from their craft to manage for themselves and provide for their needs.
And furthermore, in order to give alms to their needy brethren from
the earnings of their craft. This was the intent of the Lord.

For this reason the great Paul (when we speak of Paul, we speak
of Christ, as Chrysostom said[96]), the mouth of Christ, also understood this intent of the Lord. Not that he only worked night and day
to provide for his own needs, and for the needs of those with him:
"We worked night and day, that we might not burden any of you" (2
Th. 3:8); and again: "These hands ministered to my necessities, and
to those who were with me" (Acts 20:34), but he also commanded

---

96 Cf. *Adversus Judaeos* 4, PG 48, 866.

that whatever Christian did not work, should not eat: "When we were with you, we gave you this command: If any one will not work, let him not eat" (2 Th. 3:10). All of the divine Apostles understood this intent of the Lord, for they practiced a craft whenever they had a break from preaching the Gospel, just as they themselves bear witness to this in their *Constitutions*, saying: "For although we are occupied with the word of the Gospel, we do not neglect our additional employments (that is, handicrafts). For some of us are fishermen, some tentmakers, some husbandmen, so that we may never be idle."[97]

That everything that we have said above is certain and true and beyond any doubt is also attested to by the great Chrysostom, who says: "We should not be ashamed of crafts, or think that work is shameful, but rather, idleness and having nothing to do. For if work was shameful, Paul would not have done it, much less boast about it, saying: 'For if I preach the Gospel, that gives me no ground for boasting... What then is my reward? Just this: that in my preaching I may make the Gospel of Christ free of charge' (1 Cor. 16, 18). But if a craft was shameful, he would not have commanded that those who do not work are not to eat. The only shameful thing is sin, which is usually bred by idleness, and not only one, or two, or three kinds of sin, but every sort of evil. For this reason a certain wise man shows how idleness teaches every evil, and speaking about slaves he says: 'Put him to work, that he may not be idle' (Sir. 33:27). For what the bridle is to the horse, work is to our nature. If idleness were a good thing, the earth would sprout forth everything uncultivated and untilled; but it does no such thing... For this reason Paul was always working, not only during the day, but also at night, as he cries out: 'We worked night and day, that we might not burden any of you' (2 Th. 3:8).

And he didn't work simply for pleasure and recreation, as many of the brethren do, but he worked so hard, that he was also able to help others: 'These hands ministered to my necessities, and to those who were with me' (Acts 20:34).

He was a man who had authority over demons, who was a teacher of the entire world, who had been given responsibility

97   Book 2, ch. 63; SC 320, 336; ANF (07), 424.

for everyone on earth, and who greatly cared for and looked after all of the churches of the world, and for the people, and for the nations, and for the cities, working night and day, not ever getting tired of his labors. While we, not having the smallest bit of his responsibilities (and it is better for us not to even think about it), continually live without doing any work.

Tell me then, what defense will we have, or what apology? From here all of the evils of the earth have come, for many think that it is the greatest thing not to practice their crafts and the worst criticism to have it known that they know some craft. And Paul certainly was not ashamed to use a knife, and to sew leathers, while at the same time speaking to those in high places, but he even boasted of this, and indeed while he labored many great people of renown came to him. And not only was he not ashamed of his trade, but like some copper column, he even made it known to all through his epistles... But we, who are not even worth his shoes, are ashamed of the things which he boasted about, and every day we err, neither changing our opinion, nor thinking that this is shameful of us, that while we live by our just labors, we reject them like some enemy and laughable thing. So what hope of salvation, tell me, will we have? For he who is ashamed, should be ashamed of sin, that he opposes himself to God by doing something that is inappropriate, but he should boast of his crafts and his work.

"By being occupied with our labors we will remove evil thoughts from our mind, and we will help those who have need, and we will not knock on others' doors, and we will fulfill the law of Christ which says: 'It is more blessed to give than to receive' (Acts 20:35). For this reason we have hands, to help ourselves and those who are cripple, by offering of our own whatever we can. Otherwise, if someone remains idle while he is healthy, he is more pathetic than those who suffer from fever... There is nothing, absolutely nothing that will not be destroyed by idleness... Now that you know all these things well, how dangerous idleness is, and how much gain there is to be had from work, let us flee from the first and let us pursue the second, that we may pass the present life honorably and help whoever has need from our own possessions."[98]

98 *Salutate Priscillam at Aquilam* 1.5, PG 51, 193-196.

CHAPTER FIVE

Concerning the Story of the Magi

Some criticize us because, in the aforementioned book, *Spiritual Exercises*, we wrote about the story of the Magi and about the wonders that took place in Persia on the day that the Lord was born.[99] We will offer a brief apology concerning this, explaining that we were motivated to write this story because we see it witnessed to by many.

1) By Philip the presbyter of the Christians who, in addition to the other stories which he wrote, also gathered the oracles of the Greek seers which spoke about Christ.

2) It is witnessed to by the *Homily on the Birth of Christ* attributed to John of Damaskos. The teacher Nikephoros Theotokes verifies that this homily is authentic in the second volume of the *Octateuch*, which enumerates the unpublished books of John of Damaskos, and includes this work among them, which begins: "When the spring had arrived." But also in the first volume of the works of John of Damaskos, the following is written in the prologue to this homily: "A *Homily on the Holy Birth of Christ our God*, by the least of monks John of Damaskos, compiled from the explanation of Patriarch Anastasios of Theoupolis concerning the events in Persia."

---

99   Translator's note: See the longer Meditation 22 (also see footnote 87 above).

3) This story is witnessed to by Patriarch Anastasios of Antioch. And besides this, this story is found in almost all of the libraries of the monasteries on the Holy Mountain and of the other monasteries in the world. It is certainly found in the libraries of the monasteries of the Peloponnes, namely the Monastery of the Holy Forty Martyrs and the Monastery of Bourkanos, as we were told by the monks residing there and who have read it.

4) Last in order, but first in authority, this story was accepted by an entire Local Council gathered in Persia.[100]

In the Monastery of Great Lavra, and in the newly coenobitic Monastery of Konstamonitou, one Synodical Tome, in manuscript form, is found, upon which is inscribed: "Anastasios, Patriarch of Theoupolis: Explanation of the events in Persia." In this Tome, then, is written that while Arinatos of Persia was reigning, and Anasargaros was Consul and Diokles was Satrap, when the importance of the leading wise man of the court, Aphroditian the Philosopher, occupied an office, there was a dispute among Greeks, Christians, and Jews concerning faith. Wherefore, the king sent forth a decree, and more than one hundred bishops, and many archimandrites, from his domain gathered together. The aforementioned Patriarch of Antioch, Anastasios, was also called to the Council, for the bishops, priests, and Christians residing in Persia were subject to him. These bishops were wise, virtuous, confessors of the faith, and wonder-workers, namely, Bishop Irenaeos, Bishop Hesiod, Bishop Sechrantianos, and above all, the most-holy Kasteleus, the president of the priests and bishops, who had power and authority over unclean spirits.

When this Council had gathered, and the aforementioned Aphroditian the Philosopher was seated on the throne, regarded as worthy by the king to question and to respond to all, then some oracles of the Greek seers were brought forth from the book of the abovementioned Phillip the presbyter of the Christians, which oracles prophesied about the name of the Theotokos, Mary, saying that this name consisted of two seventy-sixes, that is, one hundred

---

100 Translator's note: This story is also reported by Julius Africanus (*Narratio de iis quae Christo nato in Persia Acciderunt*, PG 10, 97B-108D); ANF (06), 127-130.

and fifty-two – for that is the numerical value of that sweet name.[101] Upon hearing those oracles, Aphroditian began to relate the whole story he knew, just as it is found translated in the *Spiritual Exercises*. When the entire story had been told to the Council, the Tome relates that the Council did not oppose it, but all glorified God and sent up thanksgiving to Him, Whose graces were also confessed by the mouths of Gentiles and of unbelievers. This is what is written verbatim in the Tome: "And when these things had been related by Aphroditian, the entire Council was silent, for no one had anything to say to these things. The only thing said was: 'Glory to Thee, O Christ, Whose graces are confessed by every mouth.'"

So from this we conclude that, if this story was made-up and a myth, it certainly would not have been accepted by such a Council, composed as it were of such holy and wise bishops, but, rather, it would have opposed it. But if someone says that what the story writes is improbable – for how can idols dance, and the demons rejoice on account of the birth of the Savior? – to this we reply that, yes, they both dance and lament, they both take courage and become fearful, and they suffer from offensive passions, both contrary to and according to nature. But how do they suffer these things [to dance and rejoice]? Voluntarily? No. But involuntarily, forcedly, and constrainedly, being compelled by the almighty and inescapable power of God, which whips them invisibly like a whip of divine righteousness, causing them to say and do whatever they do not want to. The demons do not want to say the truth because they are the fathers of lies, and they do not stand in the truth, as the Lord said.[102] But, compelled, they shout the truth: "I know Thee Who Thou art, the Holy One of God" (Mk. 1:24). And again: "These men are servants of the Most High God" (Acts 16:17). And again: "Jesus I know, and Paul I know; but who are ye?" (Acts 19:15).

---

101 Translator's note: The name *Maria* [Μαρία] adds up to one hundred and fifty-two: M=40 + A=1 + P=100 + I=10 + A=1 is 152. Furthermore, 1 + 5 + 2 = 8, eight being the symbolic number of the future and eternal day of the Lord (see, *Concerning the Prerogatives of Sunday*, above). Curiously (or not), the name *Jesus* [Ἰησοῦς] adds up to eight hundred and eighty-eight: I=10 + H=8 + Σ=200 + O=70 + Υ=400 + Σ=200 is 888.

102 Cf. Jn. 8:44.

A demon does not want to be subjected to men and to lift any weight, because it is prideful and power-loving. But when a demon was commanded by St. Averkios, it submitted and, with loud groans, placed upon its shoulders an exceedingly heavy altar. Then, overloaded like some donkey, it transported it from Rome to Hierapolis, as we read in the *Life* of St. Averkios on the twenty-second of October. We also read in the *Synaxaristes*,[103] on the fifth of March, that St. Konon received such authority over demons, that he sent some to cultivate the earth, some to care for fruits, and some he shut in earthen pots, placing marks upon these vessels. In like fashion, the demons residing in the idols of Persia did not want to outwardly show that they were rejoicing on account of the birth of the Master, nor did they want to be destroyed and confess their defeat and their destruction. But being compelled by the power of the One born, they rejoiced, they were destroyed, and confessed their defeat. Wherefore they said: "That which is written has come upon us. As many apparitions as we have done, we have done until now, for from henceforth we are unable to do them. Whatever we have ruled, we have ruled, for from henceforth we rule no longer. We are no longer able to give oracles and prophesies. Honor has been taken from us, we have become insignificant and worthless. Only One has assumed the proper honor."

We also add this. Everything that was just mentioned, the demons can only do superficially, that is, under the force and great compulsion of God's almighty power. But they cannot do these things interiorly, that is, voluntarily and willfully, by the consent of their free will. Wherefore, even if they say that they believe: "Even the demons," says James the Brother of God, "believe and shudder" (Jas. 2:19), their faith is not an unhesitating consent to the commands of God, as Basil the Great defines faith.[104] And even if they confess the truth, and even if it seems from some outward appearances that they rejoice, or that they submit to God, all these things are done by compulsion, and by force, and without the consent of their free will.

---

103 Translator's note: The *Synaxaristes* is a book (or usually books) which contains the *Lives* of the Saints.

104 Cf. *De Fide* 1, PG 31, 677D.

Let us explain this more clearly. Even if the demons outwardly appear to believe, they are inwardly faithless. Even if they outwardly appear to confess the truth, they inwardly reject it and lie. Even if they outwardly appear to be rejoicing, they inwardly are grieving. Even if they outwardly appear to be submissive and obedient, they inwardly are insubordinate and disobedient. Even if they outwardly appear to be conquered and humbled, they inwardly are prideful. It follows, then, that this faith is not counted as righteousness unto them, because it is forced and unwanted. It is not like the faith of Abraham which was counted unto him as righteousness, as it is written: "Abraham believed God, and it was reckoned to him as righteousness" (Rom. 4:3; Gen. 15:6). And neither does their involuntary confession of the truth, nor their compelled joy and submissiveness profit them at all or assist them towards salvation. But neither are the things which the demons say virtues at all, not having been chosen by them. For that which is compelled and forced is not virtue. Hence, the demons do all these things only outwardly, and not inwardly; forcedly, and not voluntarily. There is nothing worse than the misery of the demons.

And the witness of the divine Gregory Palamas of Thessaloniki does not contribute a little to this subject. For in his explanation of the Gospel reading of the sixth Sunday of Luke (Lk. 8:27-39), he says that the legion of evil demons: "Were compelled to approach, and to submit, and to speak reverent and true words towards the Lord, confessing that He is the Son of the Most High God... And the Lord tolerated their confession unto the instruction of those in the boat. For when the disciples saw such miracles take place at sea, they said to one another: 'What sort of man is this, that even winds and sea obey him?' (Lk. 8:25). For then they learned 'what sort of man' He was, that He is the Son of the Most High (when the demons confessed this, that is). For the devil is also always an accessory to the will of God, although he himself does not want to be, nor is he even aware of it. Wherefore one of the Godbearing

Fathers[105] said: 'The devil works evil unto good, without a good intention.'"[106]

If someone says that these things are improbable, we reply that whatever similar things are recorded in ancient books and stories are therefore also improbable, like those things which Apollo said in Daphne to his false priests, in order that they might report what was said to them to Julian the Apostate, as it is written in an Ecclesiastical History: "Tell the Emperor: the statue has toppled to the ground; Phoebos no longer has a dwelling, nor Daphne a prophet, nor a speaking spring, and the babbling water has been quenched."[107]

What the enemy of the Christians, Porphyrios, said is improbable: "And now they wonder that for so many years the plague has attacked the city, Asklepios and the other gods being no longer resident among us. For since Jesus began to be honored, no one ever heard of any public assistance from the gods."[108] The entire book written by Plutarch, *On the Silence of the Oracles*, is improbable. And that which Cassius Dio writes is improbable, that prior to the birth of Christ, lightning struck the Capital of Rome and melted many idols (including the one of Zeus which was placed on a high column), along with the statues of Remus and Romulus the brothers.[109]

And whatever Symeon Metaphrastes writes in the *Life* of the Martyr Artemios is improbable, that St. Artemios declared to Julian the Apostate through the oracles of the seers that Christ is God. In brief, every other wonder which occurred before the birth of Christ, during the birth of Christ, and after the birth of Christ which indicates the destruction of the demons, and presents the power of the Godhead of Christ, is improbable.

And what should we do with what Basil the Great says, who asserts the following concerning the Magi in his *Homily on the Birth*

---

105 Makarios the Great, *De Custodia Cordis* 12, PG 34, 833A.

106 *Homily 50*.

107 John of Damaskos, *Passio Sancti Artemii* 36, PG 96, 1284D.

108 Eusebios of Caesarea, *Praeparatio Evangelica* 5.1, PG 21, 312C.

109 Cf. *Historiae Romanae*, Book 37.9.

of Christ: "And perhaps perceiving the decreasing power of the adversary and its abolished activity by the appearance of the Lord, they (the Magi) further witnessed to the great power of the One born, and by this they found the Child and worshipped Him with gifts."[110] For with these words Basil, the Revealer of heaven, basically verifies this story. And because the Magi could tell that the power of the demons had become impotent, and for this reason their idols were toppled and crushed, having been shown this, they set off from a great distance and came to worship the newly-born Master.

We close this chapter by saying the same thing that the more recent Augustine Kalmetes excellently noted concerning a separate matter. Namely, that if we allow for the possibility that certain things (like those concerning the idols) crept into the Story of the Magi, it does not, however, follow that the essence of the matter is untrue, and that the entire story is false and made-up.

---

110 *In Sanctam Christi Generationem*, PG 31, 1469B.

CHAPTER SIX

Concerning the Mystery of the Divine Eucharist

Some slander us and say that we believe the Mystery of the divine Eucharist, that is, the immaculate body and precious blood of the Lord, to be passible and subject to corruption, and that the whole body of the Lord is not in every part of the sanctified bread, nor the whole blood in every part of the sanctified wine. But those who say such things are ridiculous. For they should have read the prayers we composed and arranged in stanzas, dedicated to our Lord Jesus, which were published in the year 1796 in our book *Aoratos Polemos* [*Unseen Warfare*]. Then they would have learned what we believe concerning this subject. But, because they have become blind and have not read those prayers, we present here verbatim what we wrote there concerning this subject, unto the everlasting shame of those who unjustly criticize us.

We write the following on page 334 of the aforementioned book: "Revealing a mystery to initiates, O my Jesus, Thou didst leave a pledge for a mortal race, changing the bread into Thy very body at the supper, and the wine into Thy very blood, and Thou didst command them to do this in Thy memory. And I am sanctified by frequently partaking of these, which are incorruptible, and being deified I cry to Thee...." And further down, on page 335, we write the following: "Jesus, the One wholly in the whole Mystery and wholly present in every part of it, I confess to Thee that I approach

Thy Holy Table without the necessary preparation." Behold the pious mindset we have concerning this incomprehensible Mystery. And we not only believed, and do believe, these things, but wrote them with our very own hand. And we not only wrote these things, but printed and published them, not one year ago, or two, or three, but over ten years ago, as if we foresaw how some envious people would rise up against us to slander us. So we anticipated these things and have shut their babbling mouths with these words. And even though they are but brief words, they are sufficient to muzzle those slanderers, as they contain the whole spike and brunt of the refutation to their slanders, if I may put it in this way.

However, in order to place a bridle on their lips, behold what we add further, in abundance:

To better understand and summarize what has been said, and in order to show what we believe about this Mystery, we refer here all of the constitutive distinctions and characteristics of the divine Mystery of the Eucharist into two general and universal definitions, from which all the others can be derived.

We believe unquestioningly with our heart, and we confess with our mouth unto salvation, and we write with our hand to further convey that: First, the all-immaculate body of the Lord and His life-giving blood are actual; and second, they are spiritual. They are actual because the bread set forth on the Holy Table is, after the sanctification, truly the body of our Lord Jesus Christ, which is not a different body now than it was then, but the same. Likewise, the wine in the chalice is, after the sanctification, truly the life-giving blood of the Lord, which is not a different blood now than it was then, but the same. And because there is not one body and then another, but actually one and the same, it follows that the sanctified bread is the body of the Lord—the body actually conceived of the Holy Spirit, the one actually born of the Virgin, the one actually baptized, the one which actually suffered, the one which was actually crucified, the one which was actually buried, the one which actually resurrected, the one which actually ascended into the heavens, the one which is actually seated at the right hand of the Father, and the one which will actually come to judge the living and the dead.[111]

Wherefore, Meletios Syrigos said:

In our Holy Liturgy we remember the entire economy of Christ, remembering and hymning with a voice of praise His birth, His preaching of the Gospel, the holy passion, the Cross, the taking-down from the Cross, the third-day resurrection, and the ascension into the heavens. Yet all of these things we do over the bread which is set forth.

And in the 17th chapter of the two Councils convened against Cyril Loukaris, in Constantinople and in Jassy, the following is written:

In the Sacred Rite we believe that our Lord Jesus Christ is truly and actually present. So, after the sanctification of the bread and the wine, the bread is changed, transubstantiated, converted, transformed, into the true body of the Lord, which was born in Bethlehem of the Virgin and Theotokos Mary; which was baptized in the Jordan; which suffered; which was buried, resurrected, ascended, and is seated at the right hand of the Father; and which will come upon the clouds of heaven. And the wine that is converted and transubstantiated into the true blood of the Lord is the very blood which was shed for the life of the world by the Lord when He was suspended upon the Cross.

From this it also follows that the Mystery of the Eucharist is a true sacrifice and a perfect offering, in which Christ Himself is both the Sacrificer and the Sacrificed, and the Receiver of the sacrifice together with the Father. He is the Priest and the sacrificial Victim, the One Who offers and is offered and for Whom the offering is accomplished. Wherefore St. John Chrysostom said: "As then while Christ is offered in many places, He is one body and not many bodies; so also is He one sacrifice. He is our High Priest, Who offered the sacrifice that cleanses us. That sacrifice we also offer now, which was then offered, and which cannot be exhausted."[112] The body and

111 Cf. Nicholas Cabasilas, *Sacrae Liturgiae Interpretatio* 27, PG 150, 425C-425D; *A Commentary on the Divine Liturgy*, 70.

112 *On Hebrews* 17.3, PG 63, 131; NPNF (V1-14), 449. Concerning this, see also *Dodekabiblos*, 807.

blood of the Lord in the Mystery are also spiritual. For even though they are actual and true (as we said above), they are not, however, physical, or visible, or wholly sensible, but they are spiritual. This is understood in two ways. First, in that the body and blood of the Lord in the Mystery are acted upon and sanctified, not by any natural physical means, but by the almighty energy and power of the All-holy and Perfecting Spirit. Hence, this Mystery is supranatural. It is sacramental. It is incomprehensible. And it follows that it is beyond words and inexplicable and is accepted only by faith.

Second, the body and blood of the Lord in the Eucharist are spiritual insofar as they are not perceived according to the mode of the human body, but according to the mode of the soul, which is spirit, as Meletios Syrigos says. From this it follows that, just as the spirit, that is, the soul, is invisible and not discernable by the senses, so also the body and blood of the Lord in the Eucharist are invisible and not discernable by the senses, being beyond the senses. For the same Meletios Syrigos says: "Neither do we believe that the body of the Lord is visible and entirely sensible throughout, but we say that it is hidden beneath the covering of the bread, and that it is invisibly present in the Eucharist."[113] Wherefore some abuse the term "actual," wanting a sensible slaughtering of a body, and a sensible spilling of blood in the Mystery of the Eucharist. But if this were the case, we would also have to visibly bring in all of the sensible instruments used in this slaughter and in this spilling of the blood of the Lord, namely, the Cross, and the nails, and the spear, and the rest. But

---

113 Translator's note: St. Cyril of Jerusalem says: "For the body is given to you in the form of bread, and the blood is given to you in the form of wine" (*Mystagogiae* 4.3, SC 126, 136; NPNF [V2-07], 151). And St. Nicholas Cabasilas says: "It is the body of Christ which is the substance which lies beneath the appearance of bread" (*Sacrae Liturgiae Interpretatio* 32, PG 150, 440D; trans. *A Commentary on the Divine Liturgy*, 81). According to St. Ephraim the Syrian: "The body was the veil of Thy splendor... and the bread is the veil of the Fire that indwells it" (*Hymnem de Fide* 19.2-3, CSCO 154, 72; trans. Hieromonk Alexander Golitzin, *Et Introibo ad Altare Dei* [Thessaloniki: Patriarchikon Hidryma Paterikon Meleton, 1994], 367). St. Gregory Palamas says the same: "For this bread is like a veil concealing the Divinity within" (Homily 56, *Hellenes Pateres tes Ekklisias* [*Greek Fathers of the Church*], vol. 11 [Thessaloniki: Gregorios ho Palamas, 1986], 406).

this is not the case, it is not so. For even if the sacrifice of the body of the Lord in the Mystery is actual, it is also spiritual, that is to say, it is mystical, invisible, and beyond the senses, wherefore it is also called a bloodless sacrifice. For the Mysteries demand faith, not the senses.[114] From this it follows that just as the spirit, that is, the soul, is wholly present in the whole body, and wholly present in every part of the body, so also in the Eucharist is the body wholly present in the whole bread, and wholly present in every part of the bread. The same is to be said of the blood, which is wholly present in the whole wine, and wholly present in every part of the wine. From this it follows that just as the spirit, that is, the soul, remains incorrupt after the corruption of the body, likewise the body and blood of the Lord remain incorrupt after the corruption of the bread and the wine. From this it follows that just as the spirit, that is, the soul, being one, is divided indivisibly into all of the members and parts of the body, and is distributed undividedly, in the same manner the body and blood in the Eucharist are divided indivisibly into all the parts of the bread and the wine, and are distributed undividedly. Wherefore it is said: "Broken but not divided; forever eaten, yet never consumed."[115]

---

114 Translator's note: According to St. Cyril of Jerusalem: Be careful so as not to consider them as mere bread and wine, for they are the body and blood of Christ according to the received declaration of the Master. For even if the senses suggest this to you, yet let faith assure you. Judge not the matter from taste, but from faith be unquestioningly convinced that you have been deemed worthy of the body and blood of Christ. (*Mystagogiae* 4.6, SC 126, 138; NPNF [V2-07], 152) And St. John Chrysostom says: "It is called a 'Mystery' because we do not believe what we see; for we see one thing, but believe another. Such is the nature of our Mysteries.... I do not judge what is apparent by sight, but by the eyes of the mind" (*On 1 Corinthians* 7.1, PG 61, 55; NPNF [V1-12], 34). St. Ambrose of Milan says the same thing: "We must not look at the things which are seen, but at the things which are not seen.... Believe, therefore, that the presence of the Divinity is there" (*De Mysteriis* 3.8, SC 25[bis], 158, 160; NPNF [V2-10], 318).

115 Translator's note: These are the words said by the bishop or priest in the Divine Liturgy when fracturing the sanctified bread (the body of the Lord) just before preparing the gifts for Holy Communion.

Hence, in the year 1195, during the reign of the Emperor Alexios, the brother of Isaakios, a certain monk named Sikyditos asked: "So is the body of Christ incorruptible in the Mystery, just as it was after the passion and the resurrection, or is it corruptible, just as it was before His passion and death?" Following this, I say, those of a correct mindset brought forth testimonies from Cyril, Chrysostom, Gregory of Nyssa, and Eutychios of Constantinople: "The body of Christ in the Mystery is incorruptible, because it is that post-resurrection impassible body, not the pre-passion passible one. And whoever receives a part of the bread, receives the whole Christt, [116] and, in a strange manner, partakes of the divine Theurgy unto life eternal." Moreover, they brought forward examples from the abovementioned Eutychios, saying:

Even if someone only receives a part of these, he wholly receives the whole holy body and precious blood of the Lord, for it is distributed undividedly throughout on account of the immixture. It is just as a seal, the impression of which is imparted to everything that receives it, while the seal itself remains of the same quality and is unaltered, even if a great number of items are sealed (that is, even though the impressions are many, the seal remains one and is not many). Or it is as a voice, which goes out and is dispersed into the air: It is whole before it is expelled, it remains whole in the air, and it is deposited in all who hear it, no hearer receiving more or less than the others. Rather, it is wholly indivisible and complete and real in

---

116 Notice that they say how one "receives the whole Christ," showing that
those who commune in the Mysteries receive the whole Christ, the divinity and the humanity, and the soul and the body. That is to say, they receive
the perfect God and the perfect man, because Christ is both perfect God
and perfect man, according to John of Damaskos and all the sacred theologians. [Translator's note: That "the whole Christ" is present in the smallest particle of the sanctified bread is also attested to by St. Symeon the
New Theologian: "You should suspect nothing physical, nor conceive anything earthly, but instead see this bread with spiritual eyes, and see that
this little particle is made divine, and has become altogether like the bread
which came down from heaven, which is true God, both the bread and
drink of immortal life... the whole Christ Himself" (*Ethical Discourses* 3, SC
122, 428; trans. *On the Mystical Life*, vol. 1, 133, 134).]

the judgment of all, even if the hearers are thousands in number or greater.[117]

And Samonas of Gaza[118] and Gennadios Scholarios[119] liken the body of the Lord in the Mystery to a most understandable model, a mirror. For just as the whole sun appears in an intact and unshattered mirror, and also in every piece of a shattered mirror, in like manner the whole body of the Lord is present in the whole, unfractured bread, and also in every piece of the fractured bread. The same Samonas says:

When the sanctified bread (which is the all-holy body of Christ) is fractured into pieces, do not consider the immaculate body to be divided, broken up, or disunited, for it is immortal, incorruptible, and never exhausted. But, rather, believe that after the sanctification there is a division of only that which is sensible, unto the strengthening of faith; for a present, visible sign of the things to come; and as a pledge of and provision for life eternal.[120]

And the divine Chrysostom says: "Let us now then draw near with faith (to the mystical Eucharist, that is), all who have an infirmity. For if they that touched the hem of His garment drew from Him so much power, how much more they that wholly possess Him?"[121] And John of Damaskos says in the prayer before Communion: "And I, deplorable though I be, dare to receive Thy whole Body; may I not be consumed."[122]

We also add this, that in addition to the other slanders, those slander-loving brethren also accuse us of this, namely, that we carry around with us under our hat an *artophorion*[123] containing the

---

117 *Sermo de Paschate et de Eucharistia* 2, PG 86², 2393C. See *Dodekabiblos*, 807.

118 Cf. *De Sacramento Altaris*, PG 120, 832A.

119 Cf. *De Sacramentali Corpore Christi* 1, PG 160, 365B.

120 From the *Sacred Catechism*; *De Sacramento Altaris*, PG 120, 832C.

121 *On Matthew* 50.2, PG 58, 507; NPNF (V1-10), 302.

122 *Deprecationes*, PG 96, 817A–817B; trans. *A Prayer Book for Orthodox Christians* (Boston: Holy Transfiguration Monastery, 2000), 351.

123 Translator's note: The *artophorion* (also known as a pyx or tabernacle) is a liturgical vessel kept on the Holy Altar Table, in which the sanctified Gifts are stored for special needs, such as communing the sick.

holy bread, and that wherever we wish, whether on the road or somewhere else, we sit down and commune. When we heard these obvious and transparent slanders for the first time, we could not help but laugh; or, rather, we derided their hatred for the brethren. For we have every liberty, if we examine ourselves in accordance with the words of the Apostle,[124] having thus prepared, to enter at any time into the Temple of God and receive Communion from the priest. So what need do we have to carry around a holy *artophorion*? Let those haters of the brethren be sated from their slanders against us. The Judge is near, to Whom they will have to give account concerning their schemes against us, their fabricating of things which do not exist.

All these things we confess and believe concerning the incomprehensible Mystery of the divine Eucharist. And as many that say that in the book *Concerning Frequent Communion* we wrote that it is good for Christians to receive the divine Mysteries frequently with the proper preparation (as many Christians, that is, as are not under a rule and do not have an impediment), with the aim of eventually receiving the whole Christ—because, communing only once, they do not receive His whole body—those who prattle these things against us, I say, are the mouth of the devil, through which the devil speaks as many things as he puts into their hearts. For we are so far from this heretical opinion that such a thought—indeed, even the slightest idea and suggestion of such a thing—has never entered our imagination. Wherefore we say that which was said by Susanna: "O eternal God, Who dost discern what is secret, Who art aware of all things before they come to be, Thou knowest that these men have borne false witness against us" (Sus. 42).

As an addendum we also say this: We are so opposed to the abovementioned opinions—that is, that the Mysteries are corruptible, and that the whole body of the Lord is not present in all of the parts of the sanctified bread—that, having heard that someone was planning on publishing a work containing them, we wrote to a certain sacred individual in order to prevent its publication and thus stop public prattlings and false rumors about the most-divine

---

124 Cf. 1 Cor. 11:28.

Mysteries, since such a work would greatly disturb the Church of Christ and mortally wound the simple brethren, who do not hold to such things. And those good brethren [our accusers], getting a hold of our letter, opened it. They opened it, read it, and adulterated it, adding to it the words, "and I say the above," in order by the addition of these words to defame us as heretics and unorthodox. But may God be blessed, Who catches the wise in their deceits, according to Job.[125] For the above addition was so careless that almost all the wise teachers of the Holy Mountain saw this machination and evil creation for what it was. Wherefore, with one voice they confessed and do confess that the above phrase is an addition and an adulteration, for it has no place there syntactically according to the rules of grammar. After this misrepresentation, those grave-robbers also made copies of the adulterated document and disseminated it to many places, hoping to condemn us as heretics and to give us an evil name.

Are such things proper to Christians? Can such wickedness go any further? But would that God never reckon these things unto them. Rather, would that the Lord enlighten them and give them prudence, so that they might desist from such things and amend their ways.

As time went on, we saw and heard that many brethren were being hurt by reading this improperly opened and adulterated letter of ours. For this reason, and having been persuaded by others, we went before the Common Synaxis of the Holy Mountain and petitioned for the correction of this issue. The letter mentioned below was given to us, stamped with the seal of the Community of the Holy Mountain and signed, and it was read in the famous Church of the Protaton in the hearing of all. The letter reads:

"Most reverend Fathers and our beloved brethren in Christ living in asceticism on the Holy Mountain—in the sacred monasteries, in the sketes, and in the cells—we greet all of you with a brotherly embrace in Christ. There is nothing higher than love, and nothing sweeter than peace. For love is the sign and the distinguishing mark of the disciples of Christ, and peace is the inheritance of the Master

125 Cf. Job 5:12–13.

Christ that He left to us who believe in Him, for "peace I leave with you; My peace I give to you" (Jn. 14:27). But the common enemy of the human race and originator of every evil, the devil, does not cease warring against these two chief virtues, love and peace, and those who obey his will cause hate instead of love, strife instead of peace. Why do we begin by saying these things? Because three years ago, in this place, the most wise and learned teacher Nikodemos sent a letter to a certain sacred and spiritual individual with reference to a private subject. Some perverse and warped individuals of a crooked mind took this letter into their hands while in Constantinople and opened it and read it. This is something most unlawful, something most destructive to the political society of man, and subject to the same sentence as that of grave-robbers, according to the wise Synesios.[126] And, indeed, it is condemned by the imprecations and curses of the Great Church of Christ: Wherefore a Patriarchal and Synodical Letter was issued under Patriarch Jeremiah, subjecting anyone who would open and read a foreign letter to the severest curses. So: it was not enough for those perverse individuals to merely open this letter of Nikodemos and read it, but they also adulterated it, giving it a wrong meaning, and they copied this adulterated letter and disseminated the copies to many places on the Holy Mountain. To what end, and for what purpose? To defame the distinguished Nikodemos as a heretic and as unorthodox. Wherefore, when Nikodemos learned about these things, he came before our Common Synaxis and confessed everything that the Catholic and Eastern Church confesses, showing himself to be innocent, and not guilty of any of the accusations brought against him. And he showed that those who were defaming him were liars and slanderers. For this reason all of us, the Presidents of the twenty sacred monasteries, through our present sealed letter, notify all of the brethren living in asceticism on the Holy Mountain—in the sacred monasteries, in the sketes, and in the cells—that the aforementioned letter of Nikodemos was wrongly opened, wrongly adulterated, and wrongly misrepresented, and that copies of it were wrongly disseminated to many parts of the Holy Mountain. For

---

126 Cf. *Epistola* 142, PG 66, 1537B.

such machinations and schemings are not proper to Christians, and especially to monks and preachers. From this day forth, we decree that this much-mentioned letter of Nikodemos be void and considered as invalid and nonexistent, wherever it may be found; and this applies also to its copies. And as many as have a copy of it are to burn it and not read it, nor wrongly take information from it in order to defame the aforementioned Nikodemos.

For we all with one voice proclaim and confess him as most pious and most Orthodox, and as one nourished by the dogmas of the Church of Christ, as is evident from his sacred books which benefit all in common, in which books not a single heretical opinion is contained. And just as we confess him to be Orthodox, so should all of you come to understand this, as it is the truth. And if someone after these transpirings is provoked by that adulterated letter, and opens his mouth and speaks unjustly and slanderously against the teacher Nikodemos, he will openly be reprimanded. And he will not only be severely disciplined by our Common Synaxis, as being subject to it (being in the order and list of the Holy Mountain), but also completely exiled from this sacred place as a breeder of scandals and a lover of disturbances, and as a common enemy and corrupter of the common peace of the Holy Mountain. Everyone then must take heed to his own profession and be at peace. For, all of you being at peace with one another, the God of peace will be with you, keeping you above every encompassing circumstance. Through the intercessions of the Lady Theotokos, the especial Guardian of the Mountain, and also our Patron."

Written on July 13, in the year 1807.

+All of the Presidents
of the twenty sacred monasteries of the Holy Mountain.

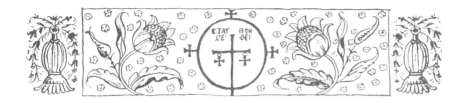

CONCLUSION

We were motivated to write these things, not in order to cause a scandal in the Church of Christ – God forbid! – but chiefly and first of all to show that we are not guilty of any of the defamations and accusations which the good brethren allege against us, and especially because they called us heretics and unorthodox, and masons. For we are not greater than the holy ascetic Abba Agathon who, when accused of being a fornicator, prideful, a chatterbox, and a defamer, received those accusations with thanksgiving. But when he was accused of being a heretic, he did not tolerate that defamation, and responded to his accusers saying: "I am not a heretic." And as an apology for this he said: "The first ones (sins, that is) I ascribe to myself, for this is beneficial for my soul; but heretic (the name, that is) means to be cut off from God." These things are written in the manuscript, *Paradise of the Fathers*, compiled by Palladios, Bishop of Helenoupolis.[127] Beloved, you must believe us; we did not set out on our own to write these things. But the key of the good brethren who criticize us opened our door, and their defamations and accusations gave birth to our Confession and Apology.

For an ancient custom prevails in the Church of Christ, that whoever is accused of something concerning the faith has every right to compose a Confession of his Faith, and to offer an apology

---

127 Translator's note: This 'saying' of Abba Agathon is also found in the *Sayings of the Fathers* (*Apophthegmata Patrum* A, 5, PG 65, 109B-109C; *The Sayings of the Desert Fathers* [Kalamazoo: Cistercian Publications, 1984], 20-21).

concerning those things of which he is accused, to assure and correctly inform those who do not have full knowledge of the issues, and to correct those who are criticizing in full knowledge, just as many and innumerable examples of personal Confessions have been preserved in the sacred books. Thus the divine Gregory Palamas composed his personal Confession of Faith, for he was being accused of being a ditheist by the Barlaamites and Akindynites. Thus the divine Cyril of Alexandria, in his letter to Bishop Akakios of Melitine, defends some bishops of Phoenicia who were being unjustly criticized for drafting a statement of their Confession. Moreover, the divine Mark of Ephesos seems to allow for this in the Council of Florence.[128] Thus also have many newer teachers composed Confessions, like Eugenios Boulgaris, and others. Wherefore it follows that no one should be scandalized seeing our own personal Confession, which is founded upon the reason given previously.

The second reason upon which it is founded is the hatred which our accusers foster in their heart against us, and against all of the brethren who keep the tradition of the Church of performing

---

128 See our footnote to Canon 7 of the Third Ecumenical Council in our
   Pedalion [pp. 173-176] concerning this. [Translator's note: The most relevant part of this footnote is the end, which reads as follows: "We have said
   all this with reference to the common Symbol of Faith [called the Nicene
   Creed]. But for anyone to set forth his own personal belief in a private confession (and let it be supposed to be in the form of a creed of his own), this is
   not prohibited, since from the beginning and down to this day the Fathers
   have been making confessions of what they personally believed, and especially those returning from heresies and under suspicion. For this reason,
   the divine Cyril in his letter to Akakios the Bishop of Melitine goes to great
   lengths in offering apologies in defense of certain bishops of Phoenicia, who
   had been criticized for making an exposition of their own creed. But even
   the divine Mark of Ephesos in Florence appears to allow this. Nevertheless, such creeds, by some called personal creeds, must have the following
   six characteristics: 1) They must not diverge from the common confession.
   2) They must not conflict with the common Creed. 3) No one must be baptized in them. 4) They must not be offered to converts from heresies. 5) They
   must not be presented as the common faith in private lessons. And 6) one
   must not add anything to or subtract anything from the common Creed,
   and then represent it as his own by incorporating it in a creed of his own"
   (*Pedalion*, 176; *The Rudder*, 233-234).]

Memorial Services on Saturday, and to hopefully uproot this hatred, in co-operation with divine grace, through our Confession and
Apology. For the brethren who criticize us and those with us, do not
conduct Memorial Services on Sunday dispassionately and without
spite, and in simplicity of heart, like those who conduct them in such
a dispassionate and simple manner in Constantinople and other
cities. No. But they conduct them passionately, spitefully, and with
hatred against the brethren.

One can verify this from the following. First, because those blessed
people often happen to have vigils and meetings on Saturday. However,
they skip Saturday, and do the Memorial Services on Sunday. Why?
To purposefully spite those who do not do them on Sunday. Second,
because the monastic life demands that monks have meekness and
an undisturbed heart. However, whenever a simple word happens
to be spoken concerning some brother who keeps the tradition
concerning Memorial Services, those blessed people immediately
become agitated, they immediately are set ablaze with anger, and
they immediately start speaking defamations against him, and
against those like him. By this they show what hatred and bitterness
they harbor in their soul. O their evils! "Who will give water to my
head, and a fountain of tears to my eyes?" according to Jeremiah,
"then would I weep for this my people day and night, even for the
slain of the daughter of my people" (Jer. 9:1). And is this not worthy
of laments? For someone to see so many brethren having left the
world, and dwelling in mountains and caves in order to save their
soul, and shedding so much sweat as if it were blood, and exerting
themselves in great struggles, fasts, vigils, hardships, bearing things
about on their back, carrying water around, and going about on
foot through rough and precipitous places, and after all this, to see
them harboring in their heart such a venomous serpent? The hatred,
I mean, against their brethren? O! Who cannot groan? O! Who
cannot but shed tears from their heart?

Wherefore we ask: Come to yourselves, most reverend Fathers,
and our beloved brethren in Christ, come, and understand the
damage which the enemy is causing you. Let go of the spite.
Uproot the hate against the brethren from your hearts, and plant

love for your brethren in them, "which is the bond of perfection," as blessed Paul says (Col. 3:14). What does "bond of perfection" mean? Chrysostom explains: "Now what he wishes to say is this: that all of those things (the virtues, that is) are bound together by love. Whatsoever good thing you might mention, if love be absent, it is nothing, but melts away. For if someone has achieved great accomplishments, whatever they may be, they are all in vain, if they have not love."[129] Fathers, abandon the defamations against your brethren, and take up praises for them, and for everyone, remembering the Apostolic word which says: "Finally, brethren, whatever is true, whatever is honorable, whatever is just, whatever is pure, whatever is lovely, whatever is gracious, if there is any excellence, if there is anything worthy of praise, think about these things" (Phil. 4:8).

We conclude our Confession and Apology with this brief, but brave and true, word. Brethren and Fathers, if you do not uproot the hatred from your heart, and do not plant love, and if you do not desist from your defamations against the brethren, know that (and forgive us for such boldness) you reside in the mountains and the hills in vain. All of your ascetic struggles and labors and sweat are in vain. Shall we say something greater? If you endure physical martyrdom for Christ, but have hatred and do not love your brethren, your martyrdom is in vain. And this is not our saying, but that of the golden minded and golden tongued John, who says: "There is nothing greater than or equal to love, not even martyrdom, which is the chief of all good works. How is this? Listen. Love, without martyrdom, makes a disciple of Christ. But martyrdom, without love, cannot achieve this."[130]

So brethren and Fathers, leaving aside the hatred and the envy and the evil defamations against the brethren, let us take up love, the sign and the distinctive mark of the disciples of Christ. And let us embrace peace towards one another, and unity and harmony, and in this way let us offer up our prayers in peace to God the Prince of Peace, Who has given us peace through the blood of His

---

129 *On Colossians* 8.2, PG 62, 354; NPNF (V1-13), 295.
130 *In Sanctum Romanum* 1, PG 50, 607.

Cross,[131] and Who grants peace to those who are far off and to those who are near, according to the Apostle,[132] glorifying with one voice, and with one heart, the All-holy Name of the Father, and of the Son, and of the Holy Spirit, the One Godhead in Trinity, to Whom is due all glory unto the ages of ages. Amen.

---

131 Cf. Col. 1:20.
132 Cf. Eph. 2:17.

ΝΙΚΟΔΗΜΟΣ ΑΓΙΟΡΕΙΤΗΣ Ὁ ΕΚ ΤΗΣ ΝΗΣΟΥ ΝΑΞΟΥ, ΕΤΩΝ ξ΄. ΑΝΕΠΑΥΘΗ ΕΝ ΚΥΡΙῼ ΕΝ ΕΤΕΙ ωΙϛ΄. ΕΝ ΜΗΝΙ ΙΟΥΛΙῼ ιδ΄. ΟΘΕΝ ΜΟΝΑΧΟΙΣ ΔΙΔΑΣΚΑΛΟΣ

Ὁ Ἑλληνικὸς Συναξαριςτὴς Μαυρικὰ Διακονι.

Ὁ Σίτω ψυχιλσ τῶν ιβ΄. Μηνῶν τῷ ἐνιαυτῷ.

Ἰωάννης Ἀντώνιος Ζ...ίδης ἐχάραξε 1818 Venezia.

,, Τίς Νικόδημος ὗτος ᾧ κλέος μέγα;
,, Ἐν ὀρθοδόξοις καὶ σοφοῖς Ὄρες Ἄθω;
,, Ὃς τήν δε Βίβλον εὐφυῶς τάξεν φιλε;
,, Νάξιος ἀνήρ. εὖγε τῆς εὐφυΐας!

UNCUT MOUNTAIN PRESS TITLES

Books by Archpriest Peter Heers

Fr. Peter Heers, *The Ecclesiological Renovation of Vatican II: An Orthodox Examination of Rome's Ecumenical Theology Regarding Baptism and the Church*, 2015

Fr. Peter Heers, *The Missionary Origins of Modern Ecumenism: Milestones Leading up to 1920*, 2007

The Works of our Father Among the Saints, Nikodemos the Hagiorite

Vol. 1: *Exomologetarion: A Manual of Confession*

Vol. 2: *Concerning Frequent Communion of the Immaculate Mysteries of Christ*

Vol. 3: *Confession of Faith*

Other Available Titles

Elder Cleopa of Romania, *The Truth of our Faith*

Elder Cleopa of Romania, *The Truth of our Faith, Vol. II*

Fr. John Romanides, *Patristic Theology: The University Lectures of Fr. John Romanides*

Demetrios Aslanidis and Monk Damascene Grigoriatis, *Apostle to Zaire: The Life and Legacy of Blessed Father Cosmas of Grigoriou*

Protopresbyter Anastasios Gotsopoulos, *On Common Prayer with the Heterodox According to the Canons of the Church*

Robert Spencer, *The Church and the Pope*

G. M. Davis, *Antichrist: The Fulfillment of Globalization*

Athonite Fathers of the 20th Century, Vol. I

St. Gregory Palamas, *Apodictic Treatises on the Procession of the Holy Spirit*

St. Hilarion Troitsky, *On the Dogma of the Church: An Historical Overview of the Sources of Ecclesiology*

Fr. Alexander Webster and Fr. Peter Heers, Editors, *Let No One Fear Death*

Subdeacon Nektarios Harrison, *Metropolitan Philaret of New York*

Elder George of Grigoriou, *Catholicism in the Light of Orthodoxy*

Archimandrite Ephraim Triandaphillopoulos, *Noetic Prayer as the Basis of Mission and the Struggle Against Heresy*

Dr. Nicholas Baldimtsis, *Life and Witness of St. Iakovos of Evia*

On the Reception of the Heterodox into the Orthodox Church

Select Forthcoming Titles

Orthodox Patristic Witness Concerning Catholicism

Patrick (Craig) Truglia, *The Rise and Fall of the Papacy*

George, *Errors of the Latins*

Fr. Peter Heers, *Going Deeper in the Spiritual Life*

Abbe Guette, *The Papacy*

Athonite Fathers of the 20th Century, Vol. II

Collected Works of St. Hilarion, Vol. II.

This 2nd Edition of

CONFESSION OF FAITH

written by Saint Nikodemos the Hagiorite with a preface
by Dr. George Bebis, translated by Fr. George Dokos,
with a new cover design by George Weis, and typeset
in Baskerville in this two thousand twenty third year
of our Lord's Holy Incarnation is one of the many fine
titles available from Uncut Mountain Press, translators
and publishers of Orthodox Christian theological and
spiritual literature. Find the book you are looking for at

uncutmountainpress.com

**GLORY BE TO GOD
FOR ALL THINGS**

AMEN.

Made in the USA
Coppell, TX
16 February 2025

46022936R00062